Praise for *Bone.*

T0031744

In *Bones of Belonging*, Annahid translates racism into easily digestible and relatable bites — which as a First Nations person I more than identified with. These inspiring, humorous, and moving stories are essential reading for anyone wanting to invest in a more inclusive planet.

— CLAYTON THOMAS-MÜLLER, author of
Life in the City of Dirty Water

If you are white like me, a book with the subtitle "Finding Wholeness in a White World," written by a person of color, might suggest a guilt trip you don't want to take. But that's not what you'll find here. Instead, you'll find a mind- and heart-opening call to help build the Beloved Community, written in a way that evokes the better angels of our nature. Annahid Dashtgard has a brave and beautiful story to tell, and she tells it with honesty and elegance in a book that's as readable as it is important. Though Canada is the setting of her journey to wholeness, she speaks directly to those of us who live and work in the U.S. "I've learned," she says, "that hope is a choice, a renewable resource." I found my own hope renewed as I read this book.

— PARKER J. PALMER, bestselling author of *A Hidden Wholeness*

As a fellow storyteller, I understand the power of story and how it can bring people together. Annahid's stories tackle racism and inequality with humour and hope in easily digestible chapters. This book is a must read for people trying to engage in authentic dialogue and action.

— ZARQA NAWAZ, comedian, journalist, and
author of *Jameela Green Ruins Everything*

We need more women of colour to speak bravely about how to take our power back. This book of stories is a road map for everything from healing our bodies to using our voices in the boardroom. It will inspire all who read it to move into action.

— DEEPA PURUSHOTHAMAN, author of
The First, the Few, the Only

In these vulnerable essays, Annahid Dashtgard gets real about her experiences of exile, teaching equity, parenting, and relationships as a mixed-race woman in a context of white supremacy. I related to so many of the stories, nodding along, marking up pages, and finding relief in her magic of meaning-making. This is a true gift to the world, a moving meditation on how we can create belonging within ourselves and our communities.

— FARZANA DOCTOR, psychotherapist and author
of *You Still Look the Same* and *Seven*

Annahid is a stunning writer, daring to speak truths that are often hidden or marginalized, and in the process opening people's hearts and minds.

— JUDY REBICK, journalist and author

In her new book, *Bones of Belonging*, Dashtgard uses the power of story to address issues of equity, inclusion, and belonging. Her essays convey personal glimpses, expressed with eloquence and humour, into her unique perspective of facing a world that needs to evolve from its current state of divisiveness and entrenched racism into a more open-minded and equitable place. Annahid's personal, passionate, and intelligent exploration of the world that she has had to navigate provides a road map that helps us all to increase our awareness and commit to doing our part in order to make our respective communities a better place to live and work.

— MARK SHAPIRO, president and CEO, Toronto Blue Jays

BONES
OF
BELONGING

BONES
OF
BELONGING

Finding Wholeness
in a White World

ANNAHID
DASHTGARD

DUNDURN
PRESS

Publisher and acquiring editor: Kwame Scott Fraser | Editor: Noelle Allen
Cover designer and illustrator: Laura Boyle

Library and Archives Canada Cataloguing in Publication

Title: Bones of belonging : finding wholeness in a white world / Annahid Dashtgard.
Names: Dashtgard, Annahid, author.
Identifiers: Canadiana (print) 20220415579 | Canadiana (ebook) 20220415692 | ISBN
  9781459750623 (softcover) | ISBN 9781459750630 (PDF) | ISBN 9781459750647
  (EPUB)
Subjects: LCSH: Dashtgard, Annahid. | LCSH: Social integration. | LCSH: Belonging
  (Social psychology) | LCSH: Race awareness. | LCSH: Equality.
Classification: LCC HM683 .D37 2023 | DDC 305.8—dc23

We acknowledge the support of the Canada Council for the Arts and the Ontario Arts Council for our publishing program. We also acknowledge the financial support of the Government of Ontario, through the Ontario Book Publishing Tax Credit and Ontario Creates, and the Government of Canada.

Printed and bound in Canada.

Dundurn Press
1382 Queen Street East
Toronto, Ontario, Canada M4L 1C9
dundurn.com, @dundurnpress 𝕏 f ⓞ

For Koda who called this book "heart-shocking" and Arion who insists a skull with flowers is really the best cover design.

DEAR READER,

NO MATTER WHO you are, this book is meant for you.

The book is organized like the bones of the human body: some pieces are longer, some shorter, some bearing more weight, others lighter in their touch. Start at the beginning, start in the middle, start at the end ... wherever you come in, the stories will take you where you need to go. The pieces overlap, one connected to another, each nudging you forward and inviting you to see, feel, and put together the skeleton of belonging holding our fragile humanity together.

I started writing this book just after Covid-19 hit us and finished as we began transitioning into a new "post-pandemic" normal. This timing was coincidental but also significant, as the pandemic became a mirror reflecting and accentuating massive gaps in access to health care, mental health support, physical safety, and opportunity based on little more than the colour of one's skin. When the murder of George Floyd saw the United States, Canada, and other nations shatter along the fault lines of systemic racism, many workplaces, organizations, and communities were no longer just looking in the mirror — they were left holding the broken pieces with no idea how to put them back together.

As someone who teaches and consults about issues of equity, diversity, and inclusion, I've come to realize that the biggest barrier to eliminating racism and other forms of systemic discrimination is that most people still don't understand the problem. When they look in the mirror, they don't know how to see these common bones of belonging within their own reflections. I hope these stories help show you our shared skeleton so you can better understand the effects of racism in ordinary life.

Fostering a world where everyone matters and belongs requires an awakening of the heart space, an extension of empathy — the ability to understand reality beyond the limits of our own experience. I hope you see yourself or others you know reflected in these stories, but mostly I hope these words kindle a desire to do better by each other regardless.

BONES

Stories are the bones of our belonging,
to ourselves,
to each other,
and to the earth.
Bones heal, hold together, carry weight, and
  endure.
Put-together bones form a skeleton in the shape of
  a body —
illuminating patterns of life and loss,
memory and dreams,
what it means to belong in and to the world.
We never escape our brokenness,
but when we tell our stories
we can make the bones beautiful.

CONTENTS

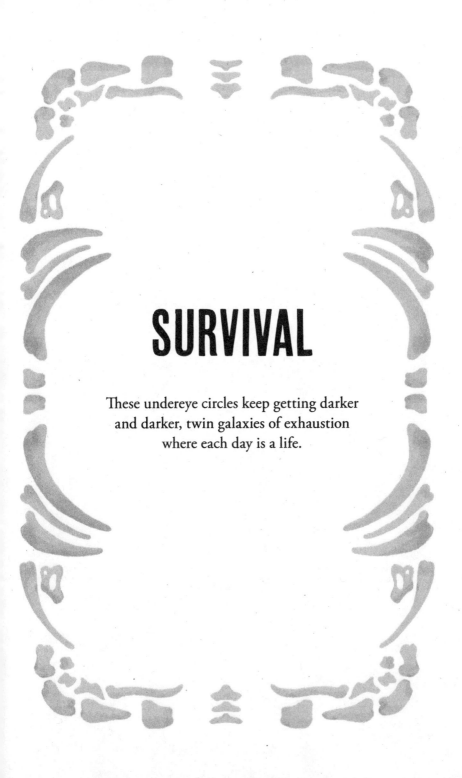

SURVIVAL

These undereye circles keep getting darker
and darker, twin galaxies of exhaustion
where each day is a life.

1

SILVER BIRCH

Month 1: March 2020

"Ouch!" I rub my head as it hits the car ceiling once again. The cottage we've rented is somewhere a few miles away on this bumpy road on the south end of the Canadian Shield, a couple hours from our city. We are surrounded by marshy swampland on either side, straight-backed trees curled like a spine around the soft belly of lake behind them. "Did you know this is moose territory?" I throw out, desperate to distract my children from their end-of-trip grumpiness. "But you have to be quiet. Wild animals don't like human noise." Their faces press to the glass and suddenly … stillness. I take a deep breath and rest my head on the window glass beside me.

"The view isn't as good on my side! I never see ANY animals. She ALWAYS gets to see them! It's not faaaaaairrr," Koda, my five-year-old son, complains loudly. And just like that, the silence is over. During this, his second year in kindergarten, he's often sullen for one reason or another. He has spent the last half year refusing to go to school each morning with no clear explanation as to why. Will this pandemic help or hurt him? I can't say. The time ahead feels like the road in front of us: slightly dangerous, with smooth passages as rare as the sighting of wildlife.

We are two weeks into isolation, introduced to a daily mutating pandemic vocabulary made up of phrases I hadn't previously known existed: Covid-19; social distancing; flattening the curve. Elderly people are dying in nursing homes across the country, unable to touch their loved ones for a last goodbye. Homeless shelters are hotbeds for transmission. Ambulances all over the world are being turned away from hospitals. We are told we will not have enough beds, enough ventilators for everyone who will get sick.

But like the layers of rocks beneath us, this is merely one strata. My divorced elderly parents live across the country — my father remarried, my mother living on her own. I am too far away to visit, never mind protect either of them. Shakil and I are two Brown people running a small business in a time where one-third of small businesses are projected to go bankrupt. Overnight, most of our work has been cancelled. We are in the middle of a house renovation with a now indeterminate end date, and the tiny apartment we rented back in the city is uninhabitable for four bodies, full-time. We are temporarily homeless and incomeless, and I'm back to first-year mothering kind of sleeping hours.

I thought exile was a thing far in the past. When I was seven and heard that we had to flee Iran, a country in revolution, for England and then, later, Canada, my illusion of safety was shattered. I remember walking in our garden in downtown Tehran repeating, "I hate Khomeini, I hate Khomeini" — taking in vain the name of the Islamic fundamentalist who had stolen our country — because

4

I needed someone to blame for our forced eviction. Overnight I lost connection to my family, community, language, and culture. Fear — deep and ongoing — branded the child I was, and so I grew up always expecting the worst to happen. I chased after the wrong boys, sacrificed health to addiction, and sabotaged happiness when it soaked in more than skin deep. It took me until mid-life to realize I was stuck in a perpetual loop, going back over and over to that moment of breakage where everything familiar was erased almost overnight.

In trauma studies, exile is placed at the top of the list of life stressors. What can be greater than forced displacement — this sudden fault line between the past, the country and place that holds who you are, and the future waiting for you, the new you that will inhabit it?

We are all in exile now.

"Look! Silver birches!" my son cries, his voice spiralling out the open window. The trees are peeling, their bark fragments like mini prayer flags waving their allegiance to Mother Earth below. Sometime soon with the coming of spring these tree skins will let go in a biologically orchestrated dance downwards. Silver birch trees shed their bark gradually, a kind of grace in action. I wonder, will I be able do the same, again?

✳

The next morning I enter the kitchen to put coffee grounds on. Since lockdown began, I've become a serial coffee and wine connoisseur, liquid bookends to each day. We are settled into a typical A-frame cottage on the Canadian Shield, this land mass over 4.2 billion years old covering over half of Canada and formerly home to volcanic mountain ranges. It's stunning to think of standing on top of more than a hundred hardened plates of lava. We've been coming here every summer and fall for over twelve years now, the familiar rock cliffs on the drive up signalling a transition to a slower pace of living. Not this time though; I can feel my body channelling these volcanic roots, erupting in emotion after emotion, and I'm waiting for the tempering effect of time to soothe all this volatile feeling into a more solid state of being.

Each day now runs a loop of routines — working, parenting, cleaning, teaching, shopping, cooking — although each of these tasks are stretched far beyond the time and energy they would usually consume. As I inhale the coffee fumes, I think back to yesterday, a typical day:

9:00 a.m.: "Put the nuts back into the container!" Shakil nags. I catch my breath before I snap the first childish response that comes to mind, "Why don't you do it?" Or better yet, the blaming version, "Do you have to be so … controlling?!"

Social media check: Hospitals across the country are frantically clearing ICU beds to prepare for Covid-19 invasion.

11:00 a.m.: "Come back here!" I yell at Koda. He always wants to avoid the reading part of his lessons, and I've run out of teacher engagement strategies, so I resort to good ol' parental enforcement. In this case it looks like chasing him around the room and grabbing the back of his shirt to yank him back to the table to finish the last page of *Days with Frog and Toad*.

Social media check: Idris Elba has the virus and is quarantining with his younger wife, who he praises as brave and resilient in choosing to stay with him.

12:30 p.m.: Carrot sticks are splayed out across the table like train tracks beside a small yoghurt lake and bread-crumb mountains. "Come back here and clean this up," I holler again at the kids. I have gone from occasional yelling mom to daily yeller. When they do a remake of the classic film *Old Yeller*, I will apply.

Social media check: Shelter occupancy is rising because of rising rates of domestic abuse. Domestic abuse deaths in some towns outpace Covid-related ones.

1:00 p.m.: Hubby and I switch places: my turn at the desk in the bedroom, chair propped in front of door to prevent kid entry (which has so far worked a grand total of two times). I try to compress ten hours of work into three hours.

Social media check: Our premier and foreign policy minister in warring political parties are now BFFs, chatting nightly to offer each other moral support.

4:00 p.m.: We have our team check-in. "We need a better project management system," one of our staff complains. I try to relax my facial muscles from betraying irritation. Can't they see how hard we are working to keep things afloat, to simply *survive*?

Social media check: A local brewery has shifted from producing beer to making hand sanitizer.

5:00 p.m.: I call my mother, who never complains, but who I can tell wants to stay on the phone beyond the ten minutes I have before racing off to resolve a quickly escalating fight between my children.

Social media check: Idris Elba again. He is now thanking healthcare staff for the excellent care he is receiving. Of course he would be; he's a movie star.

5:30 p.m.: Dinner and cleanup. A repeat of the post-lunch table landscape, this time with the addition of tiny broccoli trees. I clean up this time because it's easier than trying to chase down my kids. Plus my voice is hoarse.

Social media check: A couple of friends have written and recorded a song encouraging love and hope. I make a mental note to add it to the growing list of things to come back to later.

7:00 p.m.: Kid bedtime. After three (interminable) stories, Koda arises from the brink of sleep asking for water and wakes his sister to accompany him across the hall to get it. The trip takes twenty minutes.

8:45 p.m.: The kids are finally asleep. How the hell is this day over already? I think about meditating but need to finish some work.

Social media check: Trump is calling this a Chinese virus and claiming masks are unnecessary. (Contrary to what every scientist is saying, and anyone with basic common sense.)

10:45 p.m.: Crap, it's late (again)! I consider meditating but feel too exhausted.

Social media check: A short clip of our prime minister's daily update. I notice his beard is turning white. I note my own greys and wonder how the pandemic is accelerating their development.

2:30 a.m.: Maybe I should take some more melatonin. Sleep feels another planet away.

Coming back to the present moment I take a sip of fresh coffee, gasping as it burns my mouth. I think how tensions can so easily become battle lines in this time of in-between: partner versus partner, parent versus child, family member versus family member, co-worker versus boss. I wonder if they will also develop a vaccine to prevent the mental health fallouts from being on lockdown with double the workload and none of the usual supports. This pace feels nonstop and I can't catch my breath amid all this doing at the cost of well-being (the fact that I'm even aware of the cost to my well-being is a mark of progress made over the years through all the earlier versions of myself).

I pause from scrubbing last night's dirty pots to look out at blue lake water still suffocated by layers of white ice, like my breath held rigidly in place by a locked diaphragm. Where is the time to exhale? With a virus that is stealing our species' breath away, are we making time to breathe more deeply? Am I?

Month 2: April 2020

We're now a month and a half into social distancing, with restaurants, schools, and stores still indefinitely closed. The woods surrounding us are still covered in sheets of stubborn snow although it's approaching the end of April. I grab my thick rain jacket to go out for a walk with the little ones. Reaching the unpaved road, we decide to hike up through the birch trees. Arion, the eldest, wants to climb up the cliff in front of us, which means Koda will follow. I eyeball the slope and give my verdict. "No, it's too steep," unaware that Koda has already slipped past to go up the other side. He gets stuck halfway up so I have to clamber up to rescue him, precariously holding him as we surf back down the icy slope together. Just when I think we're home free, I hit a hidden tree root and shoot up in the air, landing right on my tailbone. Koda, often the family caretaker, runs over to me — "Are you okay, Mama?" — as he offers his hand to help me up.

Together, as we walk and hobble our way back, I hear his voice suddenly cut through the frigid air, his breath appearing like smoke. "You know, if we walk that way," he gestures through the forest to our right, "we'll reach the magical land."

"Oh, what's that?" I query, keeping my voice as neutral as possible.

"It's the place where there's no hospitals and no one gets sick," he whispers.

I feel my back clench. "Yes," I respond, "that *would* be magical." I take his hand, conscious of how small it feels in mine.

The next morning I can't get out of bed. My lower back muscles have seized, and I can't move unless bent over double at the waist, shuffling forward like a giant mutant crab. I feel closer to a hundred than to fifty, and I fear that if I move too abruptly I will dislocate my own backbone. What we are not told when thrust into the liminal space of transformation between whatever state of normal governed our lives and whatever the future will bring, is how excruciating the process can be. We're not forewarned about how we will be broken, how we will eventually be asked to surrender pieces of our past selves on the altar of the future.

I've spent most of my life reconciling the first exile, struggling to grieve the tearing out of roots just when they were anchoring in the ground. I spent years transitioning, caught between what had been and where I wanted to be: sure that who I was belonged to where I was. After this period of lockdown, we will collectively face the loss of millions of jobs and the projected worst global recession since the Second World War; we will have to grapple with the discriminatory impact of this virus hitting lower income and racialized communities with greater vehemence; we will need to find new ways of being. Will touch ever be taken for granted again? Perhaps hardest of all, we will have to learn to live with the newly awakened awareness that at any time exile in the form of another pandemic or worse could happen again. Despite how much I have anchored my life into certain kinds of emotional and financial privileges, I seem to have forgotten how none of this is security against loss, death, and the unknown.

My body, though, remembers. My body holds memory of the hostage-taking quality of fear, the heavy weight of sadness, and the restrained, yet always ready to spill over, rage. This back that has "given out" reminds me I have something to draw on: I am not in the land of exile without a compass. I hold in this body the memory of whispers of revolution, friends and colleagues taken off to prison to never return, the silent contagion of fear. The deaths in my country then were proportionally far greater than those lost to Covid in my country now. Is it not its own kind of macabre comfort that so many of us have these body memories of past exile — our own or ancestral experience — that communicate through body symptoms, reminding us of sometime past where things came apart and somehow, somewhere, we made it through? Our bones carry DNA of destruction and survival from this land that held and holds our ancestors. We are the benefactors of their resilience.

After an emergency chiropractic session, I learn there is damage to the outer ring of my lower vertebrae, the shield of my spinal column, the same microsomal horseshoe shape as this shield of land we are currently living on. This mirroring does not feel like a wholly random coincidence. Shakil bears the brunt of cooking, cleaning, and kid putdown while I sit watching, breathing through futile feelings of guilt. I know that I need to slow down and listen to my body, this patch of earth I landed in.

Despite feeling resistant, I start doing things to support my back: mini-meditations, breathing exercises, slow stretches. One afternoon lying down, I notice a rocklike tightness in my chest. I bring my attention to it, and it grows into a boulder pinning me down under its weight. Unable to move, I feel the boulder become a mountain, then a volcano spewing grief. Sobs erupt out of me for all we are losing, tears of lava flow for all who have died, for the tired earth holding us up. I cry for my son who thinks magic is someplace else but not here. I can't stop the grief once it has started, only let it run its course. Once cleared, the turmoil inside calms somewhat and as the days pass and the ground thaws, my spine gradually finds its right alignment again. The price of restoring wholeness is often vulnerability.

Month 3: May 2020

A couple of weeks later, on one of the first mornings where the sun is both shining and hot and I'm able to walk again — slowly — I pull a pile of food from the fridge. "Let's go for a walk and have a picnic!" I call to recruit the littles. Koda is the only taker. We meander together, watching frogs leap away from our approaching footsteps into puddles lining the side of the road. Monarch and tiny blue butterflies dance around our heads, and my son momentarily catches one between careful hands. When we reach the shallow part of the river nearby, I see a salmon caught headfirst under a rock, a rare wildlife sighting right in front of us. Its silver underbelly winks at me in the bright mid-afternoon sunlight and I call Koda over, thinking it's swimming upstream. I quickly realize it's the opposite. The fish is dead, the exuberant flapping of its tail to and fro caused by the fast-moving current. Spring has arrived in her full glory, and today she is showing us her prized jewels, but even here, death is an inescapable part of reality.

Sometimes, especially as I get older, I catch glimpses of the other me, the one dancing limbs akimbo in a living room in downtown Tehran, thick Persian rugs rolled aside, tables piled with trays of pulao and pistachios. I'm spinning in the centre, laughing into the faces of those crowded into the room surrounding me. Yes, a part of who we are dies in the leaving, but it's also true that exile seduces you into believing that where you left is somehow the promised land compared to the uncertain future ahead. You think the best is over and what's to come is merely to be endured. Over the years I've had to teach myself not to see dead fishes in every situation, not to search them out and turn them into whales that block the sun. I've had to learn to see the thousand shades of green, smell the hopeful mossy scent of earth after rain, and feel the solidity of the everlasting rock under my feet. Who I am today is a more sensitive and seasoned version of the person I left behind.

How do we surrender to the waves of funereal suffering while also noticing the ways life unexpectedly pops up around us like the million tiny tree buds I'm surrounded by now? During the pandemic there was unprecedented co-operation across borders to develop a vaccine. Many countries like ours offered financial life supports like the universal basic income and wage subsidy programs, and there were many accounts of wildlife frolicking and venturing into previously human-occupied spaces. There were neighbours shopping for neighbours, daily cheering sessions for health-care workers, and a flurry of free online community gatherings. There is no panacea for exile, but what we notice and nurture during these times of transformation determines who we will be on the other side — and what we will be collectively.

I notice my son's bright eyes staring up at me, tiny suns glowing in the familiar constellation of his face. After receiving so much of our attention over the last two months he is a different boy, one who giggles and chases and hugs (his daily hug quotient since the pandemic started has quadrupled). Our response to this exile will become his future resilience, and I am grateful to have a map of sorts to pass on. Drawing in a deep breath, I let it out slowly like a shooting star of love from my heart to his. The words of an old childhood campfire song drift into memory:

> Land of the silver birch
> Home of the beaver
> Where still the mighty moose
> Wanders at will
> Blue lake and rocky shore
> I will return once more ...

As I release the words into the thrumming air around us, Koda shyly joins in, hitting every third or fourth word. In this time of stolen breath, I rejoice in feeling my rib cage inflate until I am pregnant not only with unrelenting griefs but also with seeds of fragile hope, whole worlds waiting to be born.

We will return once more but it will not be to the same place we started from. Exile changes us, but it's how we deal with what we have lost and left behind that determines whether we strengthen or break.

My son and I sing loudly, rebelliously, as we walk down the rocky road atop this earth body we are lucky to always call our home. Meanwhile, silver birch trees stand bravely on either side with trunks bare, waiting like us for the restorative heat of summer.

DEAR CANADA

I've known you now for close to four decades. You and I first met when I was a scrappy nine-year-old Brown kid who arrived on your soil from Iran by way of England. Your grand open spaces shocked me after the boisterous, crowded streets of Tehran, and the more placid yet still crowded townships of England. You took my breath away with the way your prairie sky could change shades from cobalt to cerulean to midnight blue and the fact we could drive for miles sometimes without seeing anyone on the road. Your endless, unblemished open spaces, and younger culture held so much possibility. Anything could happen. I could be anyone here, *someone*.

That dream quickly died when I was made fun of, spat on at school, failed for no reason when trying for another Girl Guide badge. I stood out for reasons of both skin colour and ethnicity, and it made me very afraid to stay with you. The never-ending whiteness of your winter landscape, and of the people surrounding us, seemed like impenetrable barriers. Where was your heart, I wondered, as I closed mine off to you.

Ours being an arranged relationship, leaving was not an option. I was forced to spend more time getting to know you. Diving into shockingly cold yet serene lakes of turquoise nestled into your Rocky Mountains became second nature. I found my imagination sparked in the light-filled public library, a twenty-minute walk from my childhood home (as it was anywhere else I travelled). I was cared for through multiple hospital visits where, as a new immigrant family, we never had to worry about costs. And then there were always people who appeared like magic at times when most needed ... a superintendent who agreed to send me to a different school district; a neighbour who gifted a crocheted square, which I slept with throughout my entire childhood; a teacher who helped me create a high school chapter of Amnesty International that got me started on the path to activism. Through the thorny brambles of suspicion surrounding us, the goodness of your people found a way to seep past the protected facade I learned to put up.

As a young adult I began to travel across your vast landscape, gradually delighting in the diversity that I learned is such an essential part of who you are. I carefully picked sea-tossed pebbles off the wild ruggedness of your eastern shores while being welcomed into the homes of the most big-hearted people. I took the ferry to various Gulf Islands off the coast of Vancouver and traversed the landscape that brought the Group of Seven to fame.

The defining moments of growth for you over this last quarter century are also mine. I wept on first learning the plight of Indigenous people across this country through the Oka Crisis in 1990. I panicked at the 1995 Quebec referendum and the potential loss of one of our largest provinces. I marched in Quebec City against the Free Trade Area of the Americas agreement in 2001 with a hundred thousand others, and then again to protest Bush's invasion of Iraq two years later. I have voted in every election since reaching legal age and have organized national political campaigns sweeping shore to shore. I have talked to your media and politicians and jostled for a better, more just Canada. Over the years, you and I, we have learned to cohabitate.

I am now an adult in middle age who has found her sea legs in Toronto, marrying another of your adopted brood, a Brown boy from Pakistan who moved here, too, when he was young. Together we started a business teaching others what it means to belong. Our children attend the elementary school across from our house, and twice a year we participate in a street barbecue my husband started that has been going on for more than twenty years. Although I still live with the fear of being targeted for the ways my race, culture, and personality stand out from the norm, I have learned over time that your people's generosity outweighs their fear of difference.

I think sometimes of my ex-homeland with fondness, and other times with longing, but most of me is now rooted here. I don't know if I can say thank you for taking me in. I have also given everything I have to you. You continue to take so much, and much more from people who have inhabited this land the longest. What I can say is that I am glad to be here, waking up to you each morning, working alongside so many others to make this country a refuge for all.

Ask me which place is home, and my only answer now is you.

RAFT

Pandemic time is an ocean, one day's tides indistinguishable from the next. You hold on to the idea that you must stay afloat, though the shoreline is out of sight. I am bobbing endlessly up and down, reacting to the swells of work and kids and the unrelenting waves of dust and dishes, socks and silence. You fear drowning, so there are bursts of swimming madly in one direction or another before realizing (again) that land is no closer than before. I finally reached out for antidepressant medication. The half dose wasn't enough.

One late Sunday afternoon when the walls are closing in on me, I decide to leave the house for the first time that day, maybe that week. Groceries are a good motivator as they're needed to keep the family alive. Though I'm well insulated, the cold is shocking — its slap against my naked face reminding my body I am still here, still treading water.

No one is in the grocery store when I arrive. It's lit like a tired school gymnasium long after the games are done. I head over to the deli to see the wrapped ham and other mouth-watering delicacies behind the counter are already locked away. I want to weep at this, another lost opportunity.

The aisles stay empty as I wander through. It's comforting to realize that these shelves, with their colourful boxes of pasta and banana bunches, hold our common sustenance, shared fuel for these new lives lived completely between four walls. I may be alone but my purpose for being here is universal.

I've stretched time as long as I can. Turning the corner, there are two checkout clerks in front of me leaning on the stainless steel of their counters, dreaming, scheming, or perhaps just waiting to escape. I choose one, a young man with a bristly buzz cut and fuzzy blue mask, because he jumps up when he sees me and calls, "Come over here!"

As I'm unpacking the trolley some of the small red potatoes drop from their casing and roll across the floor. I lean down to play pick up the potatoes and notice my uncharacteristic slowness, my clumsy hands, as if I'm moving underwater.

"Do you want a new package?" he asks.

"No, it's fine," I answer.

He continues to gingerly place the three lost little lumps back with their tribe before carefully wrapping them up tight once again. "I like how you treat food," he remarks.

"How's that?" I blink, unsure what he means.

"Most people would just get a replacement. Someone dropped an apple the other day and they wanted a whole new bag."

"Hmmm," I respond, thinking of the disposability of what we perceive as flawed or imperfect. This pandemic is a selfish shopper treating all the dropped apples — the elderly, the homeless, the migrant labourers and frontline workers, anyone not white or middle class — as expendable. If I were a dropped apple, would I be picked up? Would he?

I look more intently at him, noticing for the first time his Mediterranean-looking features, the earnest diligence with which he is packing things away.

"What's your name?" I ask.

"Ahmed."

"How long have you been working here?"

"Ah ... about three weeks."

I am about to go on autopilot mode and commiserate as people do these days, saying something like "What a time to start. It must be so stressful being here right now." Instead I catch myself and query, "How has it been starting a new job during lockdown?"

He looks up, the overhead lights reflected in the amber brown of his eyes, mirrors of my own. "It's great!" he exclaims. The unexpectedness of his answer captures my full attention. "It's good to have purpose, you know?"

Leaning toward him I ask directly, "What is it about this job that feels like having a purpose?"

"Well, it's good, you know, to wake up and get out of bed every morning and have somewhere to come, somewhere where I'm *needed*." He is an apple picking up other apples before they get damaged or thrown out.

"That's wise of you," I say. He's answered a question I didn't know I was asking. I go still inside, feeling the echo of his words, and fashion them into a kind of raft. He smiles at me, and I remember how the world is not walls but water and that we never ride the waves of emotion alone. I may feel isolated but the people I'm surrounded by need me — they are my shoreline.

Under my mask, I feel my lips lift up at the corners in response. I hope he can sense my gratitude. He doesn't know it, but he gave me words to hang on to today. I pull my head above water and walk outside ready to greet the cold winter air.

NAMES

It's a furnace of a day thanks to climate change and this being the peak of summer weather. To cool off, the four of us head over to the local outdoor pool to go swimming. We have to check in at reception (a couple of makeshift folding tables) first.

When we finally reach the front of the line, the teenage attendant asks, "Names?" in a bored monotone voice, with pen poised to record them on the sheet in front of them. I suddenly get an image of immigration lines at ports of entry into this country about a hundred years ago. I always feel a slight tightening inside whenever I'm asked for my name. Still.

My son, Koda, four years old, declares in a trying-to-be-helpful and sound-like-an-adult tone of voice, "My mama's name is Ah-nah-heed. I know it sounds kind of weird, but that's *really* her name."

I laugh while inwardly cringing. From the mouth of babes! Not even my own son is exempt from the learned discomfort with names like mine, cultures like mine, ancestry like mine. Ah-nah-heed is such a common name in Iran, the Middle East, and beyond but here … it bears the stamp of foreigner, outsider, someone to be wary of. We enter the change room, and the intensive gymnastics of getting swimsuits on two hyperactive children quickly chases any memory of my own name right out of my head. Submerging myself in the cool waters of the pool is a welcome relief.

I talk to my son later that night. "That hurt me a little bit when you said my name was weird. What's different about my name versus Sally or Rachel?"

"It *sounds* different," he replies.

"But for who?" I ask. "I used to go by Anna, but then I realized my real name comes from a place where it represents water and stars, the name of a goddess, a powerful name people used to worship — and still do! It was only when I moved here that people bullied and teased me about it."

He squeezes my hand and I continue, gently. "People still get it wrong most of the time, but that's okay because now I *choose* to use it. I'd like you to use it as well."

"Okay, Mama." He nods, staring at me solemnly, his brown eyes wide and rounded in his small face.

"Thanks, baba," I whisper. Time for some hugging.

A year later, I arrive to pick Koda up from a playdate, and his friend's mother comes out to greet me. "Oh, Anna-heed," she says. "I have —"

She doesn't get any further because Koda comes out and carefully yet confidently interrupts her. "Actually, my mom's name is pronounced *Ah*-nah-heed."

I feel a little embarrassed but also … proud. He has overcome his default absorption of the norms around him because of the desire to do better by his mama.

As we walk home together, I squeeze his hand in mine, realizing I feel more than just pride or momentary self-consciousness. I feel loved.

Sometimes at busy coffee counters I will still shorten my name to Anna, just once in a while when the line is long and my time is short. If Koda is with me though, I can't get away with it. "Your name is Ah-nah-heed," he'll admonish and then loudly correct the barista as well. He has become my name guard — on the lookout for occasions where I may be slighted or minimized through the mispronunciation of my birth title. I relish how my child self is now protected by my own child, his generation learning from and correcting the erasure mine faced. Names are the first signal as to whether and how much we are welcomed anywhere. My son reminds me that a key measure of belonging will be when *all names matter.*

OXYGEN

Every couple weeks during this lockdown I visit the flower store ten minutes away. There are orange trees in the window, and in the dead of winter those little balls remind me of summer, of my homeland. I fantasize about where I could fit one of them in our plant-strewn house. Sometimes I purchase a small perennial, and I ask about care instructions, the owner responding in monosyllabic grunts as I carefully take mental notes. Nevertheless, he gruffly thanks me for my business, and in the way he gently wraps the plant to hand over to me I can tell he's glad I came.

I go on to the coffee shop next door. Only two people are allowed in at a time. Once inside, I smile back at the barista under my mask as I put in my order. I take care to put extra change in the cup and make small talk about the weather. It's the human exchange that perks me up, not the caffeine.

As I walk back home through these familiar streets of my neighbourhood, sometimes I take the long way and look at the colour of doors, the shape of clouds, and the way the light filters down on this particular day, no different than the one before it. I wave at our school crossing guard, Gabriel, an angel who shows up in every kind of weather to guide our children safely across the road, releasing them into their future safely.

This is my spiritual mealtime, this walk, as I gobble up connections to the people, objects, and neighbourhood I'm surrounded by. But sometimes I imagine myself as the mama wolf, circling the perimeters of the pack boundary, checking to make sure all is secure, that all around are taken care of. I remember that I am not the only wolf eating up these streets as I catch the eye of another on the prowl. This pandemic may be looked back on as a time of isolation, but we will also remember how we did not survive alone. Belonging has become our oxygen.

2

LION'S DEN

He looks like a mid-sixties Clint Eastwood (though less handsome) with a checked blue shirt buttoned right up to the neck, making his matching eyes pop like twin headlights on high beam. I notice him look up across the packed room and signal for the mic, clearing his throat before he gruffly challenges me. "I served in the military for many years. Afghanistan. Came back 'cause I got injured. See all these coloured folks taking our jobs ... guess I don't see how they're so special."

I pause, slightly taken aback (I haven't heard the term "coloured people" in a long time) but grateful for his honesty. My heart's beating like a runaway train, and I know this is my make-the-shot or lose-the-game moment. "Sorry, I missed your name," I respond, to establish connection but also to buy myself time to recalibrate.

"Roger," he answers. ·

"Thank you, Roger," I say, looking him in the eye, then pivoting to take in the rest of the more than sixty school caretakers packed in this fluorescent-lit room like sardines. My body feels fluid in this familiar choreography. Pausing until I have everyone's attention, I weave the usual ingredients of history, purpose, pain, and love through my body, pushing the elixir up through vocal cords, letting it out as I release the words above this rainbow sea of bodies, "I'm *so* glad you said this."

Bringing my mouth closer to the mic, I go for it: "Now shit is getting real!"

Seven hours earlier

"Shit, shit, shit, why didn't I leave earlier?" I admonish myself as I face the onslaught of early morning rush hour traffic north of the city. I'm heading into a diversity session with a group of school custodians, and I'm dreading it — for good reason. Someone inside their organization complained of our presence to a right-wing newspaper, with the article appearing only yesterday afternoon. Our work was dismissed as "nonsense," and the company we created was called a "little cottage industry created out of white guilt." Further, in case there should be any doubt as to who they were referring to, there was an accompanying (and it must be said, unflattering) full-colour photo of my heavily browed brown face hovering like a spectre above the text. This, in a context of rising hate group membership, anti-immigration sentiment, and backlash against anything smelling of political correctness, sent me to bed with very little sleep to be had.

I spent the night mentally travelling a road that took me from visions of being verbally attacked to wondering if someone might actually sneak a gun into the room to, finally, considering if someone could look up our kids on social media and kidnap them from school.

Wobbly, scared, and shaken to my core to be facing this crowd solo, I'm bracing myself to be booed out of the room. It's said that our two deepest human fears are death and rejection, but at root I feel they're perhaps the same thing. They were for me when I was growing up and I thought I might die from the pain of facing racial rejection everywhere I went. As I enter this lion's den I hope I don't get emotionally eaten up and spit out by the time the day is done. Thank God I had the foresight to stop for this second cup of coffee, scalding hot just as I like it. At times like this, it's the small comforts.

I often wonder why creating more inclusive communities is something that has to be taught, and at the same time I wonder why we don't invest *everything* we have into teaching it. Why do we have to get staff "on board" to create schools where each child can experience what the majority take for granted — a feeling of comfort when they walk through the doors, an expectation that the adults and kids around them will look after their needs, their bodies, their very lives. Sometimes I want to shake people into seeing others' realities more clearly, to just *force* them forward, to magically have humans fulfill their beautiful best selves, but the only thing I have control over is the choice to keep trying, one conversation, one group, at a time. Right now it doesn't feel like the best choice.

Three-quarters of a cup of coffee later, I arrive and pull into the school car park, relieved to be ahead of the designated start time. Leaning over to grab my black briefcase, I spill the remaining coffee into my lap. "Shit!" I yelp, out loud this time, then surreptitiously look around to make sure no one has noticed their guest speaker having a meltdown before the day has even begun. I have found it, by turns, a funny and frustrating truth that our life purpose finds us, rather than the other way around. Parker Palmer, famed educator, put it this way in his book *Let Your Life Speak*: "Before you tell your life what you intend to do with it, listen for what it intends to do with you."

When I was younger, I often tried to grab my life and shake her into telling me what she wanted of me. While I always circled around issues of race and discrimination, it took a long time for me to hang a shingle on these topics. For one thing, they are volatile and difficult areas to teach and address. Who'd sign up for that? It's also never neutral work — I have skin in the game or, more accurately, guts on the table. My role in this work often requires emotional sacrifice for group learning. Exile, immigration, and racism knocked early lessons about power, privilege, and access into these bones, so while I work to change the world I'm also working on some level to appease the younger version of myself, who is still waiting for reparations to be made. It's taken years of both study and life experience to see how the patterns of treatment I experienced when I immigrated from Iran were but echoes of a system set up to privilege white people — exactly like the group I'm about to face.

I imagine the bodies waiting behind the wall in front of me to be my nemeses in so many ways: working class, rurally living white men, the kind who decorate with *Playboy* calendars, grumble about immigration, and see Trump as their hero. It would be hard enough to face this group as an immigrant, a woman of colour, an anti-racist educator brought in to facilitate a session they are forced to attend without the article further amplifying resistance. I'm glad at least that I'm wearing black (my "I'm being serious" colour) so the coffee stain is hidden! I hope the spill is just a spill and not symptomatic of further spills, actual or emotional, to come. Mustering my inner warrior with one last deep breath, I remind myself that bravery is going forth not when things are easy, but when what you're facing feels insurmountable.

8:35 a.m.

Click-click-click, my low two-inch heels (I made a deliberate choice to not wear the four-inches in front of this group) echo across the concrete in a kind of faint but calming drumbeat. As I walk into the building, an East Asian woman with shiny, swinging black hair hurries up and introduces herself as Huang. She giggles at the end of each of her sentences. "Can I help you unpack?" [giggle, giggle]. I find her simultaneously earnest and annoying. I peg her as a fellow woman of colour who is still caught up in the internal game of moulding one's true feelings and thoughts for approval by the white men in charge. It's a familiar but frustrating reality I wish I could simply charm away. The truth is, we all put on some disguise to survive in systems where we are not represented.

"Thanks, I think I'm good," I respond. "Can you check, though, to see if the mics are working?"

As I unpack I mentally review my start. I've had all night to think this over. Teaching is like spellcasting; you have to figure out the right words, the right poignant ingredients, to mix together in the right order in hopes of capturing the room — not just the minds (easier) but the hearts (infinitely harder). The first minutes of any session are always the most important: Will people trust you enough to go along on the journey? I've decided the words to the spell for today are about values — human decency, fair opportunity, and looking after community. I figure some moral overlap is a good thing with this audience.

Grabbing my handmade makeup case with its silkscreened message *Shit I Put on My Face*, I quickly hoof it to the bathroom. Fire-engine red Ruby Woo lipstick is my special armour. All words fall from my mouth, so might as well set her up well. When I've wiped away the excess colour (I'm compulsively overgenerous) and done the thumb test so it doesn't show up on my teeth, I walk back into the now almost full hall and do a quick scan. People are jammed around rectangular tables, the backs of each set of chairs bumping against the ones behind them. There isn't much space to move and it's difficult even to take a deep breath. I feel people looking at me, some with curiosity, others with furrowed brows and straight mouths, their disdain clear. "I get it," I want to respond. "I wouldn't be thrilled attending a mandatory training either." I have learned not to take initial postures personally because if I start the day in reaction rather than invitation mode, I've broken my own spell before casting it.

I smile at Huang once more, about to ask if we're ready to begin, when a shrill voice hits my eardrums, and I turn to see a straight-haired, fit blond woman in her late forties, a mic in each hand, thrusting them toward me with guillotine-like speed. "Hiiiiiiiiiii," I equivocate, taking a step backward, unsure how to receive both instruments as my hands are already full, one with my makeup bag and the other holding my PowerPoint clicker.

"Nice to meet you!" she enthuses. "I'm Cheryl. I'm here to help with whatever you need."

I vaguely remember she does something in human resources. "Actually, Cheryl," I whisper, gesturing to the corner so I can speak with her privately, "I was really surprised to see the article in the newspaper yesterday." I pause before continuing. "Especially knowing that it was somebody inside your organization who contacted the press. It makes my job harder, and it makes me really nervous about what might happen here today." I await her apology on behalf of the organization or at least an offer of support.

"Oh … yes! The article." She acknowledges this as if she is reaching from the far reaches of her mind for the memory of it. "I wouldn't pay any attention to that."

"Well, don't you think most people here will have read it?" I ask. My job — this process of teaching people to see their biases, their prejudices, their privilege — is already not easy (to put it mildly), and the fact that all her human resources experience doesn't allow her to see that the published article will increase hostility toward me is shocking. Though, really, it shouldn't be, because part of racial privilege is minimizing impact on those who have a different identity to yourself. I am a human not feeling at all resourced in this moment.

"Oh," she laughs, "it will be fine. I'll be here in the room with you. I've booked off for the full day." I take it that I am supposed to feel gratitude for this.

I feel my shoulders tighten, a signal that rather than being supported by her presence, I sense she will be an additional liability in the room. There should be a sign on well-intentioned white women, "Beware my goodwill. I will suffocate you with it." I suppress a sigh, muster a practised smile, and say, "Okay, good. Why don't you show me how the mics work? If you can carry them around to people who want to speak, that would be helpful."

She nods enthusiastically. *And we're off*, I think. I pause to carry out a spiritual *mise en place*: "Dear Spirit, God, Mother Earth, please help me to serve the greatest good of each individual in this room and this organization as a whole." It is the start of my spell and I cast it first within myself. I have to remember I am in service of a greater vision, otherwise both the praise and the dissatisfaction sticks too hard and throws me off my game. I can't be too caught up in wanting people to like me (though no teacher/public speaker I've ever met is without this quality), otherwise I lose my ability to see what's true and what's most needed and to bring that forward for the sake of the group.

I take a deep breath, check my lipstick one last time on my phone camera, and finally turn on the mic. It's about ten steps, two metres, and one lifetime to the front of the room. "Hello," I begin. "My name is Annahid — pronounced *Ah*-nah-heed — and I'm here to talk to you about … belonging."

Mid-morning

I can tell the spell has been well cast. "I don't know about you," I started off, "but I grew up being taught to look out for others as I would my own, to treat everyone with respect regardless of where they come from or what they look like, to be my brother and sister's keeper ..." The value framing I cooked up last night worked; it caught their attention. The session has been running fairly smoothly so far, and I've just led an exercise examining stereotypes where people are invited to share their own experiences with exclusion, whether as a one-off, as part of a particular team or class group, or in an ongoing way because of the body and identity they occupy. Heads are bobbing over the tables, chairs are pulled up, and there is a tangible buzz in the room. I feel it as a palpable energy cord between the group and my own nervous system. At this point, it's hard to tell where they begin and I end. I don't take this connection for granted.

The ingredients to build rapport with almost any group of people have been wrung from moments where this wasn't so. There is nothing less terrifying than standing in front of a room of strangers — thirty or one thousand and thirty — and knowing they are not with you, that almost nothing you do or say will make them open to you, where it feels as if who you are is being slowly stripped and consumed by rows of beady eyes. We've closed the colosseums, but colosseum behaviour is still present in human beings.

I have learned the most essential ingredient to capture any group is to know my own answer as to why I am there: to choose the message over the need to be liked, to give myself permission to be real over trying to be "the right fit." I know that learning the language and rituals of belonging is the *only* way forward for our species. The undamaged version of myself and the invisible generations of children before and after me who are told they are not pretty/smart/thin/white/male/able-bodied/straight *enough* … who survive a life in exile from their true selves, haunt me. I am here to scream belonging as our common birthright. Who doesn't deserve to feel celebrated in their own skin, to find their place on this mad human journey, to know it's safe to shine brightly without being a threat to others? My battlefield is inside organizations, and the enemy (as well as the cure) is human nature itself.

I call the group back together and ask, "Does anyone feel comfortable sharing part of their experience with exclusion?" One of the few women in the room raises her hand. Her face is hard and her body is wrapped in worn denim armour. She announces, "My last principal used to call me into her office a few times each week to clean up the oatmeal she spilled from her own breakfast." Another woman sitting beside her signals for the mic to add, "*My* principal once asked me if I could go out to the parking lot and wash her car!" Her voice is vinegary, harsh and bracing. There's some scattered laughter in the room, a kind of emotional flatlining, indicating that others, too, are familiar with this entitled behaviour from superiors.

I nod in acknowledgement of her comment. "Whew," I say, injecting as much "I'm-with-you-and-feel-your-irritation-ness" as I'm able to muster. Another man, one near the back-right corner, wearing a striking blue button-up shirt, raises his hand. "I've been in this business a long time," he says, "and let me tell you, you get used to being treated like the help! Now they don't even let us talk to the kids anymore. We're not part of staff meetings. We never get asked our opinion on things." Heads start bobbing up and down vigorously, a wave of disgruntlement cresting before me.

"Uh-huh," I respond, my own head moving up and down in tandem acknowledgement. "There's a reality you're naming here about being at the bottom rung of the ladder. The invisibility, the demands, and lack of access you're describing are all ways that people who have higher positions can consciously or unconsciously take advantage. It sucks."

They are naming their experience both with lack of positional power but also having less socio-economic status — class oppression — and I know what they're describing, because I've lived it, too. When I was twenty-three, I took on a position with some status organizing a series of events for the City Hospital's centennial anniversary, while on the weekends cleaning toilets on the palliative care ward. I would be scrubbing shit one day, part of the wallpaper, spoken to as if stupid, and the next day be in the president's office giving an update on event promotions. The swing from being at the bottom of the hierarchy to being near the top was an early lesson about positional and class power that I'll never forget. Blue-collar versus white-collar, invisible versus visible, privilege of status versus the reality of social shunning.

When we wrap for lunch a short while later, I walk quickly back to the bathroom, taking longer than necessary to fiddle with my hair and fix my lipstick. "Good job," I whisper to the familiar brown-eyed, olive-brown face staring back at me in the mirror. "You can do this," I murmur, knowing the hardest part is yet to come. I slowly walk back into the room to get a plate of food for myself, to find Cheryl once again in front of me.

"Do you have the mics?" she demands, her voice like Teflon, impermeable and emotionally resistant.

"Uh … I think I left mine on the table," I answer, turning to check. The hedgehog inside me, just starting to unfurl, retreats into herself in response to Cheryl's curt tone and body language. She walks away without another word.

I shake off her abruptness.

Huang, on the other hand, comes over and I ask, "What do you think so far?" She shyly looks up at me and starts to talk in long run-on sentences, barely pausing to take a breath as if to breathe might suck up the runway for her words to land on. She describes her experience moving to Canada, how she is regularly asked to get coffee for male leaders (though it's not in her job description — is it part of *anyone's* job description?), and she has the feeling that if she disappears no one would notice. She has a strong accent so I have to lean in, and while doing so notice her eyes shifting from side to side, signs of vigilance, even with me. As I listen, I realize there is no giggling now. My window to eat is lessening, but it's part of my personal honour code to hold space for leaders of colour, leaders who have few places to speak about their experiences. I intimately know the assimilation dance of sacrificing great swaths of self in the hopes of one day discovering the magical personality combination that will unlock the door of inclusion, where getting noticed, having a voice, and being yourself can be taken for granted.

"You're going to miss lunch if you don't get in line now," Cheryl warns as she sails past again. I sigh, thinking it would be so supportive if someone (her) would offer to get the facilitator (me) a plate of food so I would have one less thing to worry about.

Mid-afternoon

I've covered the rockier terrain. Racism. Discrimination. Oppression. Privilege. These words are universes unto themselves, whole histories of billions of stories that, gathered together in one space, would rival the largest nuclear combustion. But still, I speak them as if they are words like any other, burying the investment I have in them that these words — my life — have a right to exist. They are now debriefing in small groups. We have thirty minutes left and I have to usher in the grand finale, the close of the spell. If it's left unfinished, they could all turn into frogs and I, Cinderella, will be left holding on to the tatters of my expertise.

"What insights, questions, or reflections came up in your discussion?" I ask, leaving the space open for people to lead where the group needs to go. Educating about belonging is historical reparations work as much as it is future building. The knots to untangle in every group are different. These endless conversational combinations between people — different even in the same group on another day, or in the same organization but with a different group of people — are part of what keeps me in the game. It's a constant emotional workout and it keeps my spiritual muscles strong. I scan the room for hands raised and see the same blue-shirted man who spoke earlier over in the far back corner.

"I served in the military for many years. Afghanistan. Came back 'cause I got injured. See all these coloured folk taking our jobs … guess I don't see how they're so special." There it is, a verbal bomb launched into the room that's racist but also honest. People often make the mistake of assuming experiences of exclusion translate from one group to another, like women who experience gender discrimination will automatically understand racism, or people who experience racism will be advocates for those with a disability. Sadly, this is rarely the case. Equal opportunity is a relay race where each group concentrates on running as fast as they can in a forward direction, rarely noticing the hurdles facing those travelling in the other lanes beside them. To get this group, who are holding so much justifiable anger and pain because of how they are treated as working-class people, to see and understand racism, I have to help them slow down. This man, and this group, needs to feel where they are before they can feel for others who are also on the track.

"Thank you, Roger," I say, looking him in the eye. "I'm *so* glad you said this."

I mean it.

White-collar professional spaces and people in senior leadership roles are harder to reach. It's the result of many years of training in what to say and do so that, while people may often be thinking what Roger has just said, they would never say it. In those settings I usually rely on hearsay, second guesses, whispered stories over break. But these words spoken aloud here are a gift. I slow down for a moment, drawing on years spent in therapy, on a career spanning political organizing to training in mindfulness, trauma, and conflict, as well as on ten thousand hours of conversations in spaces like this about race or gender or class or sexual orientation, with many, *many* mistakes made along the way. I exhale and step forward to wave my wand and make this moment mine, cherishing this victory of trust that someone was able to risk saying the thing that many feel but most fear speaking aloud. It's easier to call a newspaper reporter.

Bringing my mouth closer to the mic, I go for it. "Now shit is getting real!"

I don't usually swear when I'm presenting, but I follow the group. Here, speaking plainly and without the pretense of political correctness is essential. They will eat me alive or shut down the conversation at any whiff of performance. Everything I've learned is really for the courage to be vulnerable, even and especially when I'm most afraid. "Who else agrees with Roger?" I invite. All eyes are on me, and at least half of the group shoot their hands in the air, wanting in on this conversation. *I have them*, I realize. The spell I cast at the beginning of this day has worked, and the lion, if not entirely tamed, is down at my feet.

A few more voices pipe up to support Roger: frustration at people of colour getting jobs more easily or being promoted more quickly, having essentially more opportunities than white people who have lived in the country longer. I take the mic around to allow people to say their piece, the frustration in people's voices now obvious. Then, an under-thirty leather-jacketed South Asian man puts up his hand. "I was born here," he says, "and I've gone to school and church alongside people in my community, so when

I hear I got this job because of my skin ,colour, it really pisses me off." The room is silent for a beat. I can see people digesting his words. The narrative is swinging the other way. A Black man speaks up about working as a caretaker for over twenty-five years and still hearing racist slurs from colleagues, students, and teachers. Another Brown man raises his hand to say how hard he works but how isolated he feels.

The space between people speaking has increased and though there are still hands in the air, there are less of them now. It feels like the air has been let out of the balloon. A couple of years from now, this group will remember what their colleagues of colour said when they don't remember anything else from this session. I know it will make some of them think twice about what they believe and, more importantly, how they behave. I've done my job.

"Thank you," I breathe out. I feel like I've run a marathon. "We're not going to solve racism in one day — gosh, that would be convenient — but this is what it takes: for more of us to have these kinds of conversations with each other. I hope you keep it going."

4:00 p.m.

The day is finally over and I'm in an altered state as I gather my things. The magic has disappeared, leaving only exhaustion in its wake. I feel as if I could slide down on this cold linoleum and sleep for a hundred years. My bones feel like rubber, but I pull internal marionette strings to master a few more moves before I can slump into the comfort of my car. I ask Huang if she and Cheryl have a couple minutes to debrief. It is my turn to be supported and I'm hungry for some appreciation. We pull up hard plastic chairs to one of the tables in the back corner.

"Phooooof." I let myself sigh out. "What a day!" I look at each of them, waiting for their affirmation, the recognition of how much skill and bravery it took to get *this* group of people to a place of open conversation in a matter of hours, of alchemizing resistance into truth-telling — the very antidote to oppression. Huang's head is down, her eyes averted. Instead, I hear Cheryl's voice lashing toward me. "Well ... it was a little hard to hear you," she announces. I look over at her. She brazens on, staring intently into my eyes. I think there is something profound coming, and then her words sink in: "I really think you should have held the mic closer to your mouth. Like this."

I can't quite believe what I'm hearing, or seeing. She, self-appointed director of the microphone, has not heard a single word I have said. Instead of celebrating with me, she is giving me feedback on how I can become better at what she knows best, at something she is in control of. This is often the default response of the professional white woman who must maintain her own fragile sense of status at all costs. To be outdone by a man is permissible but to have a woman of colour do something one cannot do is threatening.

Just when I thought the lion was at rest, I realize it will never be gone. As Toni Morrison said in 1975, "The function, the very serious function of racism is distraction ... *There will always be one more thing*." I imagine myself grabbing the microphone from Cheryl to roar, "Do you know what it took to come here today after being personally vilified in the press by someone inside your organization?"; "Do you know that what I teach comes out of where I've been broken?"; "Would this be your response if I were a white man?" Instead, I take a deep breath and subdue the answering beast rising within my own chest.

Purpose is often talked about as the thing we cannot escape doing. As German writer Rilke put it in *Letters to a Young Poet*, "Ask yourself in the most silent hour of your night: must I [insert purpose here]?" In other words, what is it that we cannot live without doing? Less acknowledged is the price we pay for doing work that is inescapable from who we are. Teaching others about racism as a Brown person and about sexism as a woman is to constantly tend my own wounds as well as those of the world. Each moment requires digging through the internal mud pile of a million moments of invisibility and hypervisibility, of being told, or treated like, I wasn't good enough, and of the many more moments where I believed that to be true, to remember that how I'm treated is not who I am, that I can choose to keep my heart open. But what does an open heart look like right now? Do I challenge Cheryl and risk rejection or remain silent and reject myself? There is no established right place to land.

A thought comes to me. I can't get rid of the lion but I can choose the battle. Experience at the very least has taught me discernment about who is ready and who is not, and I know which side of that line Cheryl falls on. Though I feel the child in me wanting to say more to her — this white woman in authority — so that she will understand my brilliance, acknowledge my experience, thank me for my work — the woman I have become reaches for the knife and wields it as her wand to invoke one last spell, slashing through any remaining ties in the air between us. "Cheryl," I say carefully in even tones, maintaining eye contact. "I wish you could appreciate what happened here today and what it took to be here. I'm sorry you can't."

I grab my bag and stand up, glancing over at Huang as I do so. She is looking up now, her eyes wide. I rummage around in my purse and hand her my card. Whether she uses it or not, she will perhaps look in her wallet or desk drawer one day and remember me, a Brown woman who stood in front of a room of mostly white men and talked openly about race and power, perhaps lending her the confidence to one day pull away the curtain of giggles to release her own voice. "Thank you for your work," I offer before turning to leave. I realize I am really speaking to myself.

4:30 p.m.

Almost at my car, I glance back one last time to catch a flash of blue in my peripheral vision. It's Roger, leaning against the glass of the entrance door. He sees me, and I watch as his face spontaneously breaks into a smile that's like sunrise, lighting up the space between us. I grin and wave back, relishing in this sudden unexpected kinship. There's a recognition here of mutual grit, of the courage to speak it like it is, of not having the luxury to fuck around with niceties because too much is on the line. He might not yet agree with me, but I've earned his respect, and he'll be more open to the next conversation about racism. It strikes me suddenly that perhaps I was never the weaker one in this group ... I think I might be a lion, too.

DEAR DAD

I mark my Christmas visits by the piles of pumpkin seed shells you and I greedily consume together, side by side on the sofa during our annual eating competition. Holidays past you'd leave to dress up as Santa Claus, the long white beard stark against the dark brown of your face. Maybe things would have been easier here if that had been your daily outfit — at least it has familiarity going for it. Changing your name from Jamshid to Jim wasn't enough, was it?

You tried to shield me — us — from the racism we faced in this new land. Going from Auditor General of Iran to low-level accounting clerk in a government office must have been a hard swallow for you, coming from a culture and generation where male worth was judged by position, money, and success. I remember you vehemently refusing to come week after week to the white, upper-class Baptist church with us for reasons I didn't understand at the time. Years later I found out you left your job with a government ministry because of the racism you faced (although it took me more than twenty years to realize this). So often I watched you at parent night events as you stood awkwardly at the side of the gym, often alone, with a tight smile fixed on your face. Despite the hammering of these and other innumerable indignities, you never painted yourself as a victim. I wish you had. Naming racism would have taken the burden of shame off us and placed it on society. Naming something allows us to make meaning out of irrational circumstances. Now I can understand why you didn't or perhaps, more accurately, weren't able to. I really do, though I wish it had been different.

Growing up here as generation 1.5, I'm not as willing to settle for second-class citizenship, the hidden racism baked into facial expressions, marketing materials, the smug tone of people who know less but always feel entitled to tell me how it *really* is. I refuse to swallow it, and that's also because of you. You imagined the highest possible position for me, so I had big shoes to grow into. "You will be prime minister one day," you'd regularly insist, annoyed yet also impressed during our many debates (arguments) over the years. I believed you, every time. My faith in your dream for me has been my saving grace, a light that has pulled me out of the suffocating darkness many times over the years.

They say children of immigrants are less happy with their situation than their parents, because although they may not face the same battle for survival, they also expect more. It hurts in a different way, Dad, to want more and realize it's not there for the taking, that although we live in a democracy, this is nowhere near a meritocracy. That people can be good people but also hurt you by the ways they expect less but demand more. It's why I started my own company, just like you. I may not be prime minister but I am the boss. It's taken me a lifetime to shake off the dust of racism that blew into every crack and crevice, to claw a path back to the Persian girl I was when I left Iran. I've gone back to using my original name, Annahid, not Anna (not anymore). And yes, I correct people when they mispronounce it, Dad.

I wish you would stop mispronouncing it, Dad. It's okay to use my full name now.

I know to survive you made peace with the ignorant. After starting your own accounting business you needed to rely almost entirely on the goodwill of white men as your primary client base. Because you had to adapt through denial of your differences, you think speaking about race and racism is a liability, will make my life harder than it needs to be. I won't deny it, Dad, it has in some ways. It continues to make a lot of people uncomfortable to talk and teach about differences of colour and culture, identity and power ... but, Dad, you have to know that every time I watch someone shrink from the conversation, I think about you. I hope you understand that what you — we — had to swallow only makes my roar louder?

WITNESS

He's standing in front of me after our session, this tall man who works as a union representative. He softly relates the story he couldn't tell in the room earlier. He speaks of being called into a workplace arbitration where he, the only Black person in the room, had to listen as the group of white union members, management staff, and lawyers debated whether the use of the N-word was actually detrimental.

"No one approached or said *anything* to you the entire time?" I ask in disbelief.

He shakes his head, seeming both amused and resigned by my outrage. "I could only take two days of it," he muses, "and then I took a leave of absence."

I think of an earlier conversation with an older Black male friend who said to me, "I don't think about it anymore, the racism, because it's everywhere. I've learned to live with it."

"Did you say anything to leadership?" I continue.

Again he shakes his head, and I get the sense there would be no benefit in doing so.

I open my mouth to speak and decide that doing so would be a sacrilege because this is bigger than us, a shadow so big it has swallowed generations of people like him.

I hold my tongue and simply whisper, "I'm sorry."

PURPOSE

As the children tear through the living room, two and four years of age, the visiting electrician asks, "Are they both yours?"

"Yes," I answer, confused by his question, for wouldn't this be the default assumption?

He points to my son and declares, "He's a lot darker," like it's a curiosity or a curse.

I waver, unsure if I'm hearing correctly and if I am, how these words are possible within the confines of my own home.

"Yes, I suppose ..." I slowly respond, "although I don't know why it would matter."

He screws up his face, indicating that it does, at least to him.

We find our purpose in the wounded places.

The nuclear power of protective love swells up inside me, fuel for the continuing battle with these ghosts of prejudice already haunting the lives of future generations.

RACISM

It's the first session of our new Anti-Black Racism course. Our two educators have spent weeks preparing, and they start by leading the group through more than two hours of personal story, history, and conversation to paint an indelible picture of what the North American landscape looks like for Black people. In the final five minutes one of the educators tells the illustrative 2014 story of Tamir Rice: a twelve-year-old boy who was playing with his friend's pellet gun when a white onlooker called the police. Within minutes, he was murdered by a young white police officer. No charges were laid.

A Black woman in the group raises her hand to speak. She hesitantly and softly shares, "I remember Tamir Rice. I remember all those Black men before and after him. I remember them because every morning I wake up and worry if my son will be … okay. If he will stay alive. The fear gets bigger the older he gets."

Her words drop like stones among us. In the pregnant silence I recall a recent session with an executive team of lawyers, a group at the top of their field, mostly male and mostly white (the usual), their confident stances so strong yet so wrong. "We don't need to agree on racism to do something about it," one of them declared, staring me down through the screen. This from someone whose job it is to name things yet somehow can't apply it to racism — one of the most obvious and oldest patterns governing human societies. The lawyer who wins is always the one able to state the facts most clearly. I imagine they think that people being harassed, fired, or shot at because of the colour of their skin is something that happens out there, far away in dirty dark corners, the exception rather than the rule. Another person asserted, "Overall, we live in a meritocracy, and if people work hard enough, they can get here." Believing that hard work is all it takes regardless of the body or background we're born into is so comforting because nothing has to change. I recall the Brown woman saying toward the end, "I've had some of these experiences, but I didn't think it had anything to do with who I am." I suspect that group of sharp minds will just keep hiring more people of colour who will swallow the firm's colour-blind policies to keep the peace and prevent themselves from being policed. I imagine when the next shooting of a Black boy happens it will be regarded as an unlucky random act of violence.

Emmett Till. No need to name racism.

Tamir Rice. No need to name racism.

George Floyd. No need to name racism.

What world is this that people rail against a problem while denying it at the same time, a collective dissociation from truth. The energy we spend not needing to name racism is simply ... creating more racism.

There are children now who will grow up with scars — some from actual bullets, others from hurtful words and neglectful actions — who will look back at us to ask, "Why didn't they do more?"

I look into the face of the woman — mother— who has just spoken in the session, and I know she is thinking the same thing.

Why aren't we doing more?

3

BAD IMMIGRANT

The world is collectively holding its breath for the outcome of the 2020 U.S. election — Trump or Biden? Will people finally awaken to Trump's bigotry, his ruthless disregard for people's health during this pandemic, his corrupt divisiveness? I call my dad the day before the potential apocalypse — my fail-safe person to talk politics with (in addition to North American news, he consumes Iranian, British, and Russian news the way most gobble crispy bacon slices). I absent-mindedly ask if relative so-and-so in the U.S. has voted yet, and he definitively answers, "I didn't ask them. They're voting for Trump." My mind snaps to attention in shock. I know our extended family's politics vary, but I didn't expect any of them to support the dark side, especially after four years of ample evidence of what he has to offer. "They support the wall," my father explains, "to keep Mexican immigrants from coming into the country."

"But, Dad," I respond, my voice rising. I feel a hot flash coming on. "They *are* immigrants! What's the difference?"

"I asked that," he responds.

"And?" I demand, the court judge ready to grant these distant relatives instant reprieve or punishment.

"They said we're the *good* kind of immigrant."

I sit there gobsmacked, my brain obsessing over the question What is a good immigrant? And of course, good is usually measured against its opposite, so the more interesting question is What does it mean to be a *bad* immigrant? And which one am I?

There's this story we tell ourselves (especially here in multicultural Canada) that "hallelujah, we're one of the richest and most open-minded nations on earth, anyone would be lucky to move here!" Compared to most other countries, this is true. We have a high quality of life marked by free health care, one of our major political party leaders wears a turban, and people can be Canadian *and* something else. We make room for hyphenated identities — Iranian-Canadian, Pakistani-Canadian, Jamaican-Canadian, etc. — rather than force people to choose their future over their past. Yet the forced adherence to this as the *only* story can become oppressive. So many people I met after publishing my book, a story documenting the lifelong double whammy of forced departure (exile) from Iran and subsequent social rejection (racism) here in Canada, surprised me by their insistence: "But aren't you *glad* you moved here?"; "Isn't Canada the *best* place to be?"; "Look what you have been able to *accomplish*!" I started to wonder who people were trying to make feel better, themselves or me?

I wonder how many people know the other stories of those who immigrate from faraway lands — how hard it is to transplant a foreigner into the host country and hope the system doesn't reject them. Even less chance of acceptance if they come from a non-white part of the world. Dad, who was the Auditor General of Iran under the Shah's monarchy, came here to work for the Auditor General's office in the Government of Alberta. He left after five years. The reason cited: racial discrimination. I know this only because I found a file in his office drawer more than a decade later. He goes by Jim in public, Jamshid in private; speaks English with clients and Farsi at home; learned how to swallow casual racism while being the only accountant that many of his rich white clients trust.

The experience of forced immigration as a Brown or Black person, where you look like everyone else in your native country but arrive in a new one where no one in charge looks like you, is a major shock. You gamble everything to scale down to almost nothing and have little control over anything. The collateral damage is an accumulation of invisible dents and punctures to the very shape of self. You find your spirit starting to leak out. You hope you can Frankenstein yourself by grafting on a pronunciation here or adding a cultural mannerism there, but ultimately it's never enough. People sniff out the foreign in you and remain wary. Depending on what part of the world you're coming from, whether you're fluent in English, and how much money you have, the experience is either bearable or much worse. An upper-class white Brazilian has a fundamentally different immigration experience than a bearded working-class Pakistani in exile.

No, in order to have any hope of fitting in, you have to be a good immigrant, to be *grateful*, and to express this gratitude at every opportunity. To be a non-white immigrant from a non-European country requires a supersized dose of gratitude: gratitude to be here, gratitude for a better life, gratitude toward the benevolent politeness of strangers who exclude while smiling, who are able to hold on to the illusion of their inclusive politics while blocking the door to belonging. Immigrants are expected to be outwardly grateful while dealing with the anger at what they have lost and what they are facing, in private. Smile in public, rage in secret. And if you rock the boat and show any kind of anger — toward a boss or teacher, an institution or government — for expecting the same meal deal as those around you for the same amount of effort, you should just go back where you came from.

Here are the unstated rules of being the good kind of immigrant:

1. You will be renamed but always to a shrunken version of your original self, never longer, never bigger. Jamshid will become Jim and Annahid, Anna. Do not correct people, because it will be a disruption of social rank, and you should be grateful they are conversing with you at all.

2. You will hear your country's name consistently mispronounced by people who have never visited, but who will insist they are right nonetheless. "No, I'm sure it's Eye-ran, not Ee-rahn."

3. You will get asked, "Where are you from?" as the chaser question to "How do you pronounce your name?" Once people hear the answer, they will make that the most interesting thing about you or shrink back as if there is little else to say. You will negotiate relationships through your difference rather than from common ground. You will go from never thinking about what it means to be Iranian or Korean or Nigerian to creating your own mental PowerPoint ready to hit play at any time: "Yes, I was born in Iran. No, I'm not a practising Muslim. Yes, we ate a lot of pomegranates." Create the most stereotypical version of the story you can because this will be the least offensive.

4. Learn to share your birthplace sparingly, more as a bargaining chip than as everyday currency: plus

ten points if shared in a holiday icebreaker, minus ten if shared with border security. Mostly better to hide, if you can.

5. If you date someone who is white and North American born, don't expect them to understand your constant need for reassurance that you're _____ [okay, loved, secure, beautiful, smart] enough. They will not understand the insatiable hunger for something you yourself can't name but feels something like belonging, what you used to take for granted. Try Zoloft.

6. When you write a book about your life, do not be surprised when older white people look affronted: "But you're so young to —!" Just smile and pretend demureness even though they are the reason you wrote it in the first place and they will be the last to buy it.

7. When people sound surprised by, or envious of, your success — and this is important — play it down as being an accident of circumstance even though you have worked your ass off for every drop of it. They will not like seeing a Brown or Black person — especially an immigrant — rising beside or above them. Bring the conversation back to them, pretend you believe in a meritocracy.

8. When you reach a level of leadership where you are interacting mostly with white leaders, try not to act surprised or be offended when they call you "dear," comment on how pleasant you seem, ask you to do an additional five things to prove your expertise, or forget and leave your name off the session promo. People will be shocked if you bring

any of this to their attention and even more offended if you tie it to your identity, so just keep
swallowing. Again, try Zoloft.

9. Do not expect any of your friends, colleagues, or
neighbours to ask about or remember your own
cultural celebrations. If you mention that tomorrow is Eid or Nowrooz, expect a kind of benevolent glazed expression to appear but make sure to
smile appreciatively at the lacklustre, "Cool. Nice.
Hmmm," that gets thrown back at you.

10. Learn to be two different people: Canadian and
_____. You will learn to code-switch be-
tween your people and the white society you're
surrounded by, inhabiting a different self in each
place. The wear and tear this will take on you is
part of the price you pay as you pretend to belong, though your body frequently reminds you
differently.

I worry that I am the bad kind of immigrant.

✽

Just like every culture prepares tea differently, each expresses emotion uniquely. Is it sucked, hot and sweet, right onto the tongue,
or cooled with milk before being carefully swallowed? And anger,
she is the most chameleonic of them all. In Iran, she was a frequent
visitor, expressed at the dinner table over the latest revolutionary
news or because of missed dirt in the corner of the kitchen floor.
She was accepted, part of the air we breathed, how we expressed our
love for each other and the country we were part of. But in Canada,
where the status quo is modelled on emotionally repressed British

society, anger hides herself in the closet, made available only to certain people, with certain identities, over certain topics.

When I first arrived in this land of winter cold and ice, in a northern city in the most conservative province of all, I was an unruly and opinionated girl of nine. Steeped in Iranian cultural traditions of *ta'aroof* (cultural overgenerosity), of heaping tables of food wherever we went to visit, of the loud cacophony all around us, I was ... not quiet. I was also quick to express anger — "Why did you do that?!" — in a tone at least two decibels higher than necessary, only to be found a minute or two later humming or reading quietly to myself. With such ease, the emotion had no more or less hold on me than any other passing through my small growing body. But that's not entirely true. When one remembers, one has to try to remember it all.

I became more acquainted with anger than those around me, not just because of the difference in cultural expression, but also because of the deep grief and injustice I felt about our forced departure. I was seven, playing outside in our walled garden, just outside of downtown Tehran, when my father pulled me aside to tell me, "We are leaving Iran next month. The country is changing and it's not safe for us." I don't remember my reply, just the protective tidal wave of anger that rushed through me. "Why, Baba, why?!" I cried. He went on to explain, "Because someone named Ayatollah Khomeini is taking over, and he is a madman." I spent the next couple of hours tearing orange blossoms from their home branches and repeating under my breath, "I hate Khomeini, I hate Khomeini." I knew I didn't want to leave, but I also couldn't have known how much I was to lose.

By the time I got to Canada, this anger over our forced displacement had seeped more deeply into the bone and marinated into a more complicated mélange of rage, fear, and grief. But like most children, I was adaptable. If we had had a welcome reception in our new home, perhaps the rupture of soul after leaving might have healed over, to be a forgotten and distant scar on the adult shape of self. But when·we arrive somewhere as foreign bodies, as non-white bodies, racism keeps picking at the same scars, over and over again, so we stay locked in a constant cycle of hurt and recovery until survival becomes the set point.

❉

"The other children say she smells," my grade 6 teacher reports to my parents, in front of me, in the classroom, my prison. I am three years into life in Canada and have gone numb, not from the bone-chilling winters but from the emotional temperature here. I don't understand why the other children don't like me, why they cross the street to avoid me. I don't understand why people move away when I go with my father to get groceries or to the library for books. I don't understand why I am spat on, or called Paki, or, worst of all, the way I am rendered invisible by people passing by me to greet other people who look and sound like them, pale skin and thin accents. I lose faith in the adults around me to make things better because most of these adults do not seem to see what I see or hear what I hear. Like many children, I have taken belonging for granted, and now that it has been stripped away, out of my reach, I don't know where to go.

A lifetime later I will face my daughter just as she is starting school, asking me with great concern, "But if you were just moving to Canada, and we share the world, why was it so hard?" I will struggle to find a good answer.

I stop sleeping at night. A few months into our arrival, I remain hypervigilant in the darkness for hours after the lights go off. That continues for years. I desperately want to rest but am unable to surrender to a state where I feel I have no control over what happens .

to me. I am not aware of feeling much of anything, just an internal crouching, like a fox in its den, hearing the howls of the hounds from a distance. The emotion I reach for, wrap around me like a cloak of protection, is anger. Anger is safe, she is a gatekeeper holding back the less predictable monsters of fear and grief. Anger stokes the coals of hope that perhaps one day things just might change, get easier. Anger helps me hold on to the notion that I deserve to be greeted like those around me, with smiles and cocked ears, micro-signals of respect. Anger holds my hand through the long years of childhood, as much an internal parent as the ones I have outside of me who themselves are surviving this foreign territory. Anger lends me the strength to fake confidence when what I mostly feel is inadequacy.

When I'm twenty-eight and living thousands of miles from the small town I immigrated to, in the major metropolis of Toronto, I will be confronted with these ghosts of the past in the aftermath of 9/11, as I watch images of Middle Eastern people on TV and hear them speak about being called names or spat on, or about their houses or places of worship being vandalized and burned down. Overnight, Iranian immigrants have gone from being the tolerable kind of immigrants (never quite achieving model minority status like their Eastern European or East Asian counterparts) to the devil incarnate. The fragile skin of belonging that has grown over the early wounds of rejection is scraped raw. I feel both exposed and dissociated. I call my family members almost every day, unclear whether I am reaching for support or offering it. A week after witnessing the world I thought I knew being dismantled, my white landlady knocks on my door to whisper to me with mock concern, "Are you okay? I can hear you yelling into the phone. It sounds like you have a lot of anger."

Rather than abashedly apologize, this is what I wish my young adult self had said to her: "Fuck yes, lady. I am angry. I am tired of swallowing the grateful immigrant narrative when I bust my ass twice as hard and get half the recognition. I'm angry when I watch the rising racism and Islamophobia, and I realize that the tolerance of diversity Canadians pride themselves on actually masks a fear of difference, which has, like most uncomfortable truths, been swept under the happy Canadian multicultural mosaic rug, waiting, just waiting, to emerge. I am angry that people here shy away from conversations about race and immigration, identity and power, words that are my world. I am angry because I want things to change, and anger is the emotion that drives things to be different. I am angry because I don't know how else to be in the world right now. For the same reasons you can't access anger, it's all I can feel."

Maybe being the bad kind of immigrant is good for me.

Anger is an important ally in the struggle to find belonging in someplace new. But also, we can't be colonized long-term by a singular emotion. It starts to stunt our growth, becoming counterproductive. The ability to express anger freely is liberating, whereas being in anger lockdown as the way to survive racism and xenophobia is just the opposite. That moment of waking up to my anger set me on a journey to better understand it. I realized that because anger was so marginal in my adopted culture, I often felt ashamed of it and ignored what it had to teach me. Gradually, through meditation, therapy, and bodywork, I allowed the fire of anger to subside, so the waters of loss, anxiety, and fear could flow through and out of my body.

It took many years. Trauma — as a result of threatening experiences we cannot undo or escape — means that we lose our ability to know where our boundaries lie. Sometimes I overdid it and reacted to things my partner or children did that were clearly undeserving, or I underdid it in other moments, like being yelled at by a white teacher in my child's classroom as I stood numbly by. Dad, he just forged through, only to berate me through the years for being too sensitive and expecting too much. I watched him turn into an Iranian nationalist — the kind that could single-handedly appear in adverts in pro-Iran tourism videos — unable to hear any criticism of his home regime. I recognize this now as his own way of dealing with it all. Righteous anger is often a cover for grief.

Gradually, I worked at developing a relationship to anger separate from trauma, one that allows for spontaneous, opinionated expression aligned with my passionate Persian roots. For many of us, it is hard to differentiate personality versus identity: one is intrinsic and the other a response to a cultural story where we are moulded into ways of being not always of our own choosing. I didn't choose this anger: it was a by-product of survival, racism, and the weight of being sold a bill of goods that were rotten to the core. When I was a child, I believed that if I just worked hard enough, I could be prime minister one day. But the reality is that there are so few people of colour leading in hospitals, schools, and, especially, government positions. If people do succeed in getting there, they are very much the exception rather than the rule, the token non-white holding up the diversity flag. I had to make peace with this society I found myself a part of rather than constantly fighting for it to be different or, at least, choose my battles and find more sustainable ways to fight for change. I have learned that the best kind of anger has to be connected to love.

Recently, I got upset when a conference organizer asked me for my professional title, to promote me in their advertising. After giving it to them, I heard back that they'd have to check "if it was okay to use," as there was no self-promotion allowed. I was speaking for free. I swallowed and paused before responding. I let myself feel the feeling and what it was telling me. I was angry because I was feeling disrespected and because I suspected this wouldn't happen to a CEO of a bank, a white man who would never be questioned about their title or integrity. I replied via email, "I am formally declining the invite to be part of the conference. Given the time and generosity I have extended to be part of this, the level of micromanaging is not what I would expect, and it doesn't feel good to me." I moulded my anger into a boundary: no drama, no depression, just a line in the sand. A healthy relationship to anger offers a border between ourselves and the dominant story, allowing us to thrive, allowing for the possibility of relationship across a belonging divide.

❈

Belonging is often described as a kind of homecoming, being anchored to a place and claimed by its people. Black and Brown immigrants are stuck in this in-between place, sometimes for generations, haunted by a country that no longer exists, invisible to the people in the country they find themselves in. And just like any other citizens of any country on earth, immigrants *deserve* their anger. My dad, he composted his anger differently, had less opportunities to hide his differences and less skills to cope with the impacts. But both of us, all of us, deserve the right to be a bad *and* good kind of immigrant, to be angry or polite or peaceful, or any other way we choose to be, because this is what belonging comes down to: the ability to occupy our full humanity, to align who we are and how we feel with how we experience reality. If we can't exist in the fullness and ease of who we are, then our newly adopted nation — *the world* — doesn't get the best of us. We all lose out. To be good or bad or really any kind of person is an illusion, a two-dimensional image.

It has been twenty years since I was that young woman who started embracing anger as an ally rather than a liability. I'd like to say I *always* use anger mindfully and purposefully, that I have it under control, but that's not true. Anger can still be a volatile and mischievous mistress. What is truer is that, with time, I have learned to be playful with her, to be more aware of her shape-shifter nature, of her need to sometimes control, sometimes speak out, and sometimes appear when she is not needed at all. I've embraced the knowledge that she is an essential part of the stuff I'm made of and impossible to separate from — as valuable a piece of me as my heart or my courage. I will never deny or dismiss her, denounce her, or, worst of all, pretend she is not here because without anger ... I may not be.

Now when my growing daughter asks me about the past — "Why was it so hard?" — wanting to know why it was hard for me to move here when it isn't for her to grow up here, I pause and feel the years carved into this transborder body. Time has softened and rounded the jagged edges of self. I have (mostly) forgiven my country for its ongoing transgressions and (mostly) forgiven myself for ways I transgressed against myself. I answer her, taking my time: "People are learning about differences we didn't talk about then. I'm learning, too. I'm glad I get to do it *here*, with you." And after all these years I mostly, and *gratefully*, mean it.

I've become the mostly grateful kind of immigrant.

GHOSTS

It's late and I want nothing more than to go to bed. The usual nighttime demons of anxiety, loneliness, and abandonment are arriving to feast, settling in to keep me company for the night. I want comfort but it feels far out of reach. Instead I have my daughter, Arion, appear in front of me demanding a glass of milk before bed. Before I catch myself I've tumbled down the rabbit hole into the past.

I'm suddenly six years old — the same age she is now — in downtown Tehran a few months before we are forced to leave. I'm sleeping over at my friend's house for the first, and last, time. Before bed, her mother offers each of us a glass of warm milk with a single teaspoon of sugar. The spoon is silver and the lights are bright. I don't remember anything before or afterward — the shape of her house, where I slept, what her mother looked like, or the next morning. There is merely this ripe memory where my childhood self tasted for the first time a new kind of sweetness, registering it as comfort. I can't recall feeling this way after that.

As I watch Arion gulp down the warm liquid in front of me, the ghost of my childhood self reminds me of something adult me often forgets — that comfort is not found in the telling but felt through the body: the touch of a grandmother's lips blowing patience into the top of a curly haired head; cheeks pressed into a mother's warm belly; the firm clasp of a lover's hand. I reach over and take a sip from my daughter's cup, feeling the milk's creamy warmth spread across my tongue. It tastes just as pure, as sweet now, as it did back then. I feel both younger and softer.

Is it not comforting to remember that memories have the power not just to haunt us but also to heal, that our six-year-old self can bring comfort to our forty-six-year-old self, reminding her that she, too, was loved so that love can be passed on? As I get ready for bed, the demons are present but quieter. They are not the only inhabitants here. Each of us have stored in the bone access to love imprinted across borders, time, and generations reminding us we are not alone as the dark settles in.

AUNTIES

"Mmmm ... Looking so good, yah?" this Desi auntie murmurs as she gives a quick head nod of approval, not to me but rather to my gym-clad companion. I turn to look, wondering how my friend's black yoga pants and matching top outshine my fuchsia-pink suit jacket and high-heeled sandals. Is it that she's wearing more visible makeup, that she's thinner or just prettier — at least conventionally so? I should be able to shake off such moments, but they still rankle me. Why do I want to be considered the pretty one anyway?

These aunties are the life-breath of Brown culture the world over, so busy cooking, cleaning, fussing, caretaking but also, like many historically silenced groups, wielding power passively through gossip, tone of voice, a thousand gestures invisible to anyone outside the culture. They speak their own binding language of love that can slowly suffocate even its own native speakers.

I usually appreciate these aunties. They have often clucked over me, like when I was clumsily dressing in traditional clothing for the Muslim portion of our intercultural wedding. One of them spent twenty minutes on my blusher alone and longer on the correct drape of my *dhuputta* (neck scarf). These aunties act as the canary in the coal mine — they are the first to alert you if you look tired, have gained or lost weight, or aged even slightly. They will often come at the drop of a hat when asked for help, eager to outdo each other and themselves in the generosity department.

But none of this comes for free. Mostly raised in countries and generations where women were taught they could be only one way — pretty, domestic, and keepers of the family fold — they pass this internalized oppression on to us women choosing a different path forward. My generation and younger confuse the aunties with our boldness, voice, and career choices. What box do we fall into?

To fall into any grey identity area is threatening for expats already under threat of losing their root culture and ways of being. The result is perhaps a more vociferous intergenerational tug-of-war over cultural identity and expectations than ever before.

I remember when I gave birth to my first child I was introduced to the custom that the extended family comes over after twenty-four hours to welcome the new one to the family. It's a lovely idea but it almost did me in. Out of mind with anxiety and panic after an unprecedented life experience that triggered all the old trauma buttons, and physically in pain as well as bleeding nonstop, the very last thing I wanted was to play hostess to a group of thirty people. I acquiesced because at that time I still wanted to be the good girl, the good wife. But after having a sobbing meltdown in our bedroom by 7:30 p.m., after people had been swarming our house all day long, I was forced to acknowledge my limits.

There is also still the expectation that we women will shop, cook, serve, and clean up at every family or social gathering. I do my part minimally in the preparation stage and fully in the cleanup. Often Shakil, my husband, will wander in as the lone male to help. Usually though, the men sit in the living room sleepily snacking, pontificating, and watching the TV. This model may have worked when women were in charge of the domestic sphere and men in charge of work outside of it, but the women of my generation and younger work full time or more. Sometimes it's enjoyable to chat with the other women as we package food and wash pots and pans. Other times I silently seethe at the injustice of outdated traditional practices our worth is still measured by.

And perhaps hardest of all to swallow is the machine-gunning of advice from these aunties about appropriate clothing, my children's personality traits, the colour of our carpet, or the overripe bananas. It is nonstop and my ADHD brain gets spun out as I attempt to respond to one subject while being chastised already by the next. I have learned to shut up and nod and, if starting to vibrate as I feel myself shrinking, to change the topic or make an abrupt side shuffle toward the bathroom.

Raised by my father to expect to move through the world like a man, what if I refuse to give up those expectations when in Brown spaces just to fulfill the ideal of what a good woman should be? I would then be considered white, and that is akin to outsider status — even oppressor — so who wants that?

I mostly swallow and conform to these expectations by choice, because I know to do so is a sign of respect for this flock of older Brown women who get so little of it everywhere else. It's the least I can do to show some solidarity. The rest of the world demands they change the contours of who they are and how they operate, but they don't need to do that in private spaces. I also honour the sacred purpose underlining all this gendered behaviour: a tending of the collective, making sure no one is left out in the cold. Though I find it hard at times, these aunties remind me of the power of personal sacrifice in favour of community well-being, a rare attribute in the Western world, which constantly tells us to look after ourselves first. These aunties, they know that the secret to belonging is to think of others first, and though I don't always like the price I have to pay to fit in with this cultural code, I know they also put my needs often above their own.

I think if we choose the oppression we choose to live under, it is not oppression anymore but a form of service.

I glance from my friend beside me to smile back at the auntie in front of us and respond, "You look good, too!"

ROSES

I have spent too long assuming that people who are happy most of the time are innately predisposed that way by virtue of genes or through the ease of privilege. As I've gotten older, I realize how much contentment is also a choice — what we focus on, what emotions we hold onto, how we make meaning out of what happens to us.

I coach my six-year-old son, who too often answers the question "How was your day?" with "Bad. Awful. Terrible." Now that I'm on to him, I'll ask him to choose three good things before he tells me anything bad. I have various strategies to coax, tease, push these positive things out of him but mostly I tell him, "We have to train your brain to see all the good things along with the hard ones. There are usually more roses than thorns." I am trying to teach him what it has taken me half a lifetime to learn.

He tells me one day that there are *actually* more thorns on the stem than the one rose on top. He's sharp. I laugh, yet I persist.

Depression and anxiety run in both his bloodlines, stamped in through war, revolution, and exile. I worry he has inherited the generational impact of so much loss with his sensitivity and how hard he can be on himself.

What I forget sometimes is that our ancestors *also* feasted and fought, loved and laughed. They lived, they survived, they were resilient. They remind me that my job as parent is not to de-thorn my son's young life and simply hand the roses over, as tempting as that may be. What type of ancestor would that make him?

Rather, as he gets pricked, and even as the blood drips down, I want him never to lose sight of those wild pink petals yonder and above, curved gently toward the sun, always ready to receive the tender gift of light.

4

DUSTY ROAD

Relationship Year 2: Cuba

We're in Cuba on red farming soil under hot sun, much more like the countries we originate from — Iran and Pakistan — than the one we now call home. We stare at the occasional farmer and bovine-looking creature in the fields as we wander past, finally claiming scant refuge from the sun under a bare tree in the middle of a barren field (at least to my city eyes). After sitting for a few minutes, tuning into the slower rhythm of this landscape we're temporarily part of, I think to myself, *This is it*, and turn toward Shakil.

> As this girl sits under this hot sun
> she knows in her heart you are the one.
> Will you join me in the years ahead
> knowing our love can only spread? ...

This is our insider magic, these elementary rhymes belying emotional depth. He responds in kind.

> A watermelon girl you are for me,
> bored with you I'll never be.
> By your side is where I choose,
> let's place our bets where we can't lose.

For people who don't put a lot of stock in the conventional, bums on bark and sweaty hands threaded together was our knee-on-ground, diamond-ring moment.

The dusty road became our metaphor. Whenever we find ourselves in a new environment, in a bumpy patch in our marriage, facing an obstacle in front of us, he will turn to me and say, "Dusty road," which roughly translates to "We're on this path for the long haul, and we'll keep going beyond what bumps are in front of us now." It's a prayer flung to the winds for two first-generation immigrants forced from countries in conflict — me from Iran because of revolution, him from Pakistan during the East-West Pakistan civil war — to a continent on the other side of the world.

Childhood, 9 Years Old: Alberta

One Saturday morning shortly after arrival from Iran, when I still believe I can be a princess in this new land, I attend a children's craft event at the local library. We make badges with Mod Podge glue, afterward dutifully following the timid-voiced teacher's request to go around and share our results. Then, as now, I have too many words to fit into most spaces, so I go on to share the more exciting tale about my morning, finishing with "and then we were rushing so much to get here we almost left my sister behind!"

As I giggle, I notice ten pairs of eyes staring back, and then someone leans over to whisper to their neighbour, "She's weird. And she smells." The instructor says nothing, only averts her eyes before moving on to the next child. But even as the people around me, in this moment and beyond, fail to provide me with the always-hoped-for happy ending, I soon discover that the books I surround myself with could fill in the missing plot.

Two years later, I was standing outside the same room in the same library, scanning shelves for the next Anne of Green Gables book in the series. It's another story where the female lead is fated to fall in love and then get married (always in that order). Like all children, I would shape who I was by imagining myself in these worlds I encountered through books, movies, and TV shows. This narrative of "romantic love conquers all" became its own form of addiction, filling an empty space inside me hungry for social love and approval. I moved from Anne and Gilbert to Scarlett and Rhett to the entire Sweet Valley High series. I sobbed at the stories of love found and then lost: Maid Marian and Robin Hood, Charlotte and Wilbur, Anna Karenina and Count Vronsky. I grew up imagining that if someone loved me *just like that*, it would calm the wolf inside keeping me awake most nights, sometimes howling until pre-dawn hours, always on guard against attack.

I was blind to the reality that all the women portrayed are white, Christian, and homegrown (no foreign imports in these tidy tales). The fact that I am not any of these may be the very reason I consume these romantic fantasies so desperately. These stories represent a kind of cultural currency, a Norman Rockwell hangover that forms the nucleus of Western society. When the women between these fragile paper covers find love, they are desired, pursued, gifted, feted, and given a special kind of power, elevated in the eyes of their beloved. When the denominator of one is multiplied to two, it becomes a circle with belonging at the centre. Romantic love among white couples seems a sacred place where unconditional belonging exists. It became my Holy Grail.

Like many girls of my generation I pursued male attention with fervour, with an edge of desperation, because I felt this attention had the power to make or break me. In a society where most people in power are white and male, this is not surprising. Summers find me at a Christian summer camp, always accompanied by my best friend: blue-eyed, blond-haired, slim, and sweet Caroline. Days are filled with chores, crafts, and learning water sports like windsailing and canoeing. Sweet Caroline receives male attention from a number of the most popular boys — Andrew, Peter, and Paul — biblical names that never go out of fashion in white worlds. Our last summer at camp there is plenty of romantic intrigue involving her and more than one of these Herculean figures. I am fully invested in the story, but I never appear on the page. I don't even expect to.

I am there but not there. When we have been rejected from the story and don't see ourselves reflected anywhere, a part of us is kept outside of existence. These absences of self can retreat and lie dormant, but they do not, and cannot, lie in wait forever.

It becomes impossible to find peace because the void left by these absences creates a vacuum that starts to suck in everything good; the need to fill the void begins to trigger addictive behaviours. It turned out that I would cycle through different addictions in my life but this first addiction, this yearning for a rescuing of self through romantic love, was the foundational one.

Relationship Year 12 or 13: Toronto

After a decade of marriage, mid-life finds us busy and, by all appearances, living the white-picket-fence dream — two children and a house in a bustling metropolis. Yet nights often find us facing down a tunnel of clashing needs and hurt, an uncomfortable coda to our bustling days. I find that after 10:00 p.m. the old absences within become dark matter, a gravitational force destroying all love that comes my way. Facing ongoing rejection as a Brown girl for all those years has become an emotional cancer eating away at confident parts of me. Racism deprives people of the belief they are lovable. I have become a love hypochondriac.

The next morning I'm flying out to give the keynote speech at a large American conference. I've had too much wine, will not be getting enough sleep, and feel in desperate need of … something. After I've brushed my teeth and had my nightly wind-down bath, I get into bed to snuggle beside Shakil.

I can sense his slight pulling back, a kind of protection perhaps against the pull of my dark matter. It's enough to set off my rejection sensors.

"Why are you pulling back from me?" I pounce, too late wishing I had tempered my tone or refrained from commenting at all.

"I'm not!" he counters defensively. "Can't you just tuck in? I'm too tired to do any more talking."

"I didn't realize I was burdening you," I snap, triggered by the idea that the time for intimacy, which I measure by words, has passed.

"For God's sake!" he lashes back. "I don't have energy for this tonight! Can we please just go to sleep?" He pulls the blanket away as he turns over on his side.

His pulling away feels like the ripping away not just of love, but also my security in this dark world … the once-more removal of a motherland. It's a boundary I have no control over, but I try.

"Why are you turning away?

"You don't want to have any time together before I go?

"Can you tell me that you still love me?"

We both know how the road forks at this point. Either I stop and let things be or keep pushing and risk him walking away.

While I'm living my life, successful and smart, there's also *her* — this child inside who is rocking about on the ocean, trawling desperately for food, for love. Yet even when I pull up a full catch, by the time she makes it back to shore most of it has fallen through the holes. I don't know how to sew up the net or stop fishing. I want him to do what every hero does in most romance plots: rescue the princess and banish the threatening darkness forever. But in the stories, the princess doesn't need rescuing every day.

After a couple minutes of silence where I am unsure whether he has fallen asleep and I can feel myself move into a state of hyperawareness, which I know means I will be awake for at least another few hours, I hear him whisper, "Are you just nervous about tomorrow?"

I know this is his way of trying to assuage my need, of extending a hand across the void between us. "Yes," I respond, aware I am starting to drown in familiar rocky waters of grief, anger, and shame. I close my eyes briefly, wondering what my life would look like if I had all parts of myself to work with along the way. Was it immigration, the crossing of ocean, that left behind a self scattered in the water like a bread-crumb trail the adult me has spent a lifetime chasing? Was it the shock of racial rejection after arrival, people's subtle (and not so subtle) aversion of gaze, contemptuous pursing of mouths toward a child who looked and acted differently? Is there just something different neurologically about me? I sense that how I make meaning of this nightly haunting is the key to moving past it, but searching for the answer in this way, every night, feels like its own form of addiction.

"Well, I *do* love you." His tone is sincere yet tinged with annoyance. "But more importantly, you need to tell yourself."

I turn over silently, annoyed with him for not trying harder and myself for giving in once again to this insatiable need monster that seems to sabotage connection by pushing so hard for it. Why haven't I yet learned that it's impossible to expect one person to fill the country-sized hole in my heart?

Relationship Year 2.5: Toronto

I am watching Shakil tell his story to a group of strangers as part of an anti-racism session. He speaks of being five when he moves from Pakistan and starts kindergarten in Canada's steel town, Hamilton. For the first few months, while he is still learning English, he is beaten up by his classmates on the way home from school. Once, he says offhandedly, he gets a concussion, so the principal has to drive him home. He goes on to describe the usual menu of racism for most non-white kids in small town North America: the fear of smelly ethnic food for lunch; the fear of associating with any of the other Brown kids; the overcompensating behaviour that for him translated into becoming the class clown.

He has me at "beaten up." Maybe the tears running down my face are my own implicit understanding of what he had to face; maybe it's the stirring of our future son, whose tenderness is perhaps a result of these very experiences; maybe it is touching the shadow of all children who are similarly failed by the systems they trust to protect them. In the car on the way home I question him about what he shared. "I didn't know any of that. Why didn't you tell me? That's significant what happened to you!"

"It wasn't for very long," he says, "that the violent stuff happened." I internally reflect that the physical violence was probably the least of it. He goes on to say, "I don't remember it that much. And then I learned the language and was able to make friends, so it got easier."

It takes me many years to realize this downplaying of impact is his coping strategy. Individual response to conflict arises in part from family survival patterns. The model of relationship we had, like millions of other immigrant kids, was a kind of toxic codependency, where parents stayed together out of a sense of responsibility and sacrifice. When people forget that being together is a choice, the past slowly grows over the relationship, cutting off oxygen, choking off growth for everyone. When non-white immigrants from extended family contexts immigrate to white-dominant countries they often deal with one or more of the following survival patterns:

1. See No Harm: A refusal to acknowledge barriers, pushing forward to succeed regardless of cost to health or relationships.

2. Perfectionism: No emotional or psychological space for failure or mistakes.

3. Shame and Blame: When mistakes or individual preferences result in the person being judged harshly and accused of selfishness, with love withdrawn as punishment.

4. Status Cloning: Only acknowledging those that become doctors, engineers, or lawyers — status professions that cross national boundaries. Any other profession is seen as unworthy of the parent's sacrifice.

5. Worry Addiction: Endless worry over small concerns. Nothing is ever enough.

6. Hypochondriacal: A variation of habit #5 but focused specifically on *whether one is warm enough in this cold climate.* Inordinate amounts of time spent fussing over whether one has enough layers (specifically socks and undershirts), regardless of the weather outside.

7. Shroud of Silence: Whole topics, especially those connected to emotions of loss or grief, rendered out of bounds. The only version of the past allowed is the most rose-coloured version, if acknowledged at all.

8. Romanticizing Homeland: A variation on habit #7, blaming everything that goes wrong on the new country. The one left behind is rendered perfect in every way, conveniently overlooking conditions that led to exile in the first place.

9. Competing and Comparing: An inability to acknowledge that who we are is enough; constant comparisons to rich white people being the metric of success (i.e., security).

10. Denying Differences: Pretending at all costs to be more _____ [professional, funny, smart, polite] than long-term inhabitants of the country. If cultural norms are mastered, maybe racial differences will be ignored.

Although both our families held a few of these patterns to greater and lesser extents, Shakil's family specialized in a variation of #3, the *Shame and Blame* conflict coping response. This meant that when things came up, he would emotionally shut down and retreat. He had no ability to distinguish between a featherlight or steel-beam–heavy kind of conflict, and both resulted in the same strong response. On the other hand, my family was really good at #1, *See No Harm*. I learned, from my father especially, not to see barriers and that if I pushed hard enough, I could overcome anything. The end result is that I learned to become a fighter, relying on anger to fuel my change efforts, and Shakil became a peacemaker, hiding anger as a liability to being accepted.

In our dance across the conflict chasm, the more he stepped backwards, the more I would step forward — fight and flight, the oldest defence mechanisms in the books.

Relationship Year 1: Vancouver Island

Early on, I visited Shakil on the West Coast, where he was working for the summer. We went for a walk one night and stopped to
look up at the naked sky, dotted with countless bright freckles.
As we stood there together, dwarfed by the evergreens and ocean
surrounding us, he took my hand in his and started softly singing
words to an iconic Blue Rodeo song where the chorus contains the
lines "And if we're lost, then we are lost together." I didn't realize it
was a harbinger of what was to come, how we would need to master
the art of being lost together.

The language of a culture is relationship, and its currency, belonging. When these are stripped away early on through exile, immigration, or migration, and there is no ability to make sense of this loss
or to grieve it, you lose touch with this essential currency of what
it means to fully be alive and to take for granted a space to exist.

This loss — of culture, of home, of belonging — becomes
stamped into your bone marrow. It replicates itself daily through
blood and humours, amplified through interactions with family
and community, shaping reality with every word spoken and step
taken. When two people come from a past of revolution and civil
war, strewn with the deaths of friends and kin, to land in a home
on the other side of the world where the sun only seems to shine
in the windows of light-skinned people with the right accents and
clothing, the usual romance narrative doesn't apply. How can it?

Being in a relationship across broken ancestral lines has meant
examining inherited survival patterns that constrict our ability to
just *be our best selves*. In our Brown immigrant marriage, we have
invested in lots of years of therapy, together and separately, forging

new understandings of how systemic discrimination places pressure on individual relationships. We have learned to slowly disentangle our personal struggles from the failed promises of this free society, where we are supposed to be equal under the law but which neither of our families experienced in reality.

Not growing up taking equality for granted, it is no surprise that the place we have forged belonging is our shared commitment to teaching, advocating, and pushing for it. Anima Leadership, a company we co-founded and grew together, is now one of the larger inclusion companies in Canada, as well as a gathering place for people looking to be in brave conversations across race, gender, and other differences and to build more authentic relationships in the process.

I think of our work as both the result of, and reward for, staying on the long dusty road our ancestors prepared before we were born. What gets broken from one generation to the next always holds the possibility for repair, but only through the channel of relationship. To welcome the past and gradually separate the pain shadows from present-day circumstances, to discern what is our own emotional work to do and what belongs to the other person, where to draw a line and where to give in … is the hardest work because the other person in a marriage reflects not just your light but also your darkness.

Relationship Year 15: Bedroom

We've had an argument over something and have spent the last hour in separate parts of the house. I go in search of him, still the one that usually needs to re-establish connection first. I find him in the bedroom.

"Come here," he says. "Lie beside me for a moment. I'll give you a cupcake hug."

I grudgingly walk over and lie down beside him, allowing his arm to cup me. "What's a cupcake hug?"

He starts to stroke my side. "A little hug treat. Cupcake. Hug."

I fire back, "Well, I hope you're doing this because you want to and not because you think I want it."

I can hear the smile in his voice. "You came all the way up here. You might as well get a little treat for all that effort."

"You make me sound like a dog!" I exclaim indignantly.

He pauses, then queries teasingly, "In a relationship, don't we all act like dogs for each other at times?"

I swallow my words. He knows how to wrap messages for my heart in words that slip past the mental guards. I feel myself take a deeper breath and sink a little further into the pillows.

"Want to cuddle in?" he asks.

I don't reply but turn toward him, pushing him on his side so I can spoon him from behind. *No more words*, I silently remind myself, though it's hard. If I could just explain again what I meant, *why* he was in the wrong. With an internal sigh, I close my eyes. I am not at peace, but I do feel a little bit better. Sometimes appreciating the first signs of thaw are as good as it gets. Enough of me is here, I think, to let go the clutching need for now, to remember I don't need to win to love.

Over the years, the antidote I've found to quell the grasping need is to learn how to sew up the holes in my neural love net, allowing me to stop the desperate fishing for love too much of the time in my marriage. I've done this through ongoing personal therapy, through medication for anxiety and depression, through experimenting and finding ways to cultivate and hear the voice of my soul self. The more I romance *all* the different aspects of myself, the easier it is to take belonging with Shakil for granted and to notice how magnificent this ocean of human connection can be.

✳

"Look at your beautiful mama," he'll say to both kids as I walk, sometime waltz, into the kitchen in the morning (always the last one, still on Iranian time four decades later).

"I like your hair best with its wild curls — it's like your personality, it doesn't like being controlled," he'll comment in passing as I awkwardly raise the blow-dryer to quell those rascally hairs.

"Can you go do your pushy thing?" he'll plead in certain situations where assertiveness is required, both of us knowing I can out boss anyone, not a skill he excels in.

"Do you really need to say that? It didn't sound kind. You were off your game," he'll admonish after certain interactions.

"You're a writer. When you write it's like your soul comes to greet the paper," he'll say, after I read him something and look up to catch the tears in his eyes.

Compliments. Acceptance. Collaboration. Reckoning. Recognition. There are countless ways to be in a relationship and these moments of connection shift like a kaleidoscope throughout the day, more gradually through the years. What I have found is that the most beautiful, and also infuriating, gift is *how clearly this person is able to see me.* If a country and its culture was my first home, this marriage has been my most formative one.

Somewhere on the Path

"Is it me or are the birds louder this year?" I ask.

"It does seem that way," he responds.

We sit in silence watching the striations of green in the tree canopy above us.

"I'm sorry," I say for what feels like the hundredth time but also the first, because it's still hard to feel so exposed as I step into the light. "I don't know how to be in partnership, really. I always had to push to make things happen for our family growing up. It's hard to switch the settings off survival mode, but I recognize when I'm pushing I leave you behind."

He nods, and I reach out to grip his fingers in mine.

I have learned to apologize when the old darkness rises because although we both endured racism, he wasn't left in trauma as I was. The trauma is not his to fix. It shouldn't be mine either, yet it's become a part of who I am. Over the years, I have learned to hold off its grip for longer and longer periods of time, and when caught have learned how to (mostly) rescue myself. I have slowly and grudgingly learned to see that in and among the dark matter is a whole galaxy of stars, bright shining aspects that light up the sky, beautiful, not in spite of what surrounds them but because of it.

We watch as a determined robin lifts a piece of silver ribbon and carries it in her mouth to the branches above. "Look, that robin is building its home from nothing," Shakil whispers.

Our gazes follow as she fusses around, arranging the shiny thread as the base of her nest, trusting it to hold the weight of all to come.

This may not be a fairy-tale romance with a nice, tidy ending, but I don't want that anymore. We've built this nest straw by straw, truth by truth, love over love, and it's become our safe transport as we continue down the uncertain dusty road.

HALOS

Mornings in our house are marked by coffee and chaos, far from the calm I dream of daily. It's another one, not yet 8:00 a.m., and I hear my seven-year-old son yell from the next room, "You're a bitch!" (not a word we use in our house). I rush over, unsure whether to pull his provoking older sister away from the line of fire or to admonish him for his unpardonable language. I do both at the same time.

"You can't say that word! Especially to a girl or a woman!" I hiss, triggered at the thought of my son getting enlisted into toxic masculinity so early on. His small face scrunches up as he yells back, "Why not? Everyone else in my class uses it!" and with that, he spins away and stomps back up the stairs. I regret passing on the art of the dramatic exit as I watch him stealing my move.

Taking a deep breath, I decide to get my daughter out of the door and on her way to school. After three more shoe changes, a demand for her winter jacket packed away downstairs, and two more spoonfuls of yoghurt we finally get outside. I call Shakil as soon as I'm free half an hour later, after dropping her off. This is my calm time, walking through the forested ravine, our city's backbone. "Did you talk to him?" I ask.

His answer reminds me why he's my partner in equity work. "Well ... I explained *bitch* doesn't just mean a female dog ... which was his impression." I laugh at hearing my son's innocence, relieved it is still present. "Then I told him that some words are swear words and only adults can use them. And then there are other words that are hate words, and no one should use them. Of course, then he wanted to know other hate words, and you know him, he wouldn't drop it."

"Aaaaah. What'd you say?" I ask, mentally creating my own forbidden list.

"*Paki*. I told him that was one that was used against me — against *us* — growing up, and that I hope he never has to hear it."

"And?" I prompt.

He was silent at first. And then he just whispered, "Me too."

I look up at the leaves changing colour, thinking how easy it is that a word in one context becomes something entirely else in another. *Bitch*, female dog. *Bitch*, foreplay to violence. *Pakistani*, cultural group. *Paki*, racial slur. The only difference, the feeling driving them. We can't blame the leaves for falling, but we can tend to the health of the tree, watering roots with love rather than fear, fertilizing with knowledge as opposed to ignorance. Thinking of my son reminds me of what's possible when we tend to these roots day after day, year after year, generation after generation, branches growing ever closer to the sun. As I turn the corner I see the sun peeking through the treetops, transforming the boughs above me into a million tiny golden halos.

BLOOM

This hoya plant in our bedroom was gifted to us many years ago. It's held a place on our bedroom shelf for over a decade, its waxy leaves like tiny prayer flags, its branches lush green arms welcoming us into rest each night. I know this plant can flower, but despite watching it closely over these years, it never has for us.

I think how Lady Hoya has watched so much conflict in this room. The same script each night on wash, rinse, and repeat. Repeat. Repeat. Repeat. Me wanting him to fill the cavern that opens at night, thirsting for love. Him needing to close all doors to settle into refuge. Our nighttime needs for surrender echoing our earliest Brown immigrant survival patterns: I learned to push, he learned to mediate; I overcompensated, he negotiated; I spent a life searching for a replacement for loss of homeland, he spent a life building its replacement. In this most intimate space we act out the age-old survival battle to get our needs met: fight or flight, confront or retreat.

Yet over the years we have tilled the soil of our love. Repeat. Repeat. Repeat. Some relationships take longer to bloom. With him I have learned that love is something made anew every day, a choice we commit to again and again. Over the years, we have journeyed forward, he and I, exploring together what it means to belong in relationship across difference, trauma, and need. We've woven these understandings into our work in the world.

We continue walking this path, what used to be a full conflict now boiled down to a sentence or two, an insider shorthand, a line we step back from and move on.

Today, for the first time, and after two children and close to fifteen years of living here, the same time we have been together as a couple, Lady Hoya offers her first waxy pink bloom. I move closer to take her in. Like the delicate underlay of a tutu, her blossoming beauty is unexpected, yet perhaps it is not entirely random.

SKATES

It's a Saturday and our family is seated in the kitchen, pancakes in various stages of arrival onto plates. Arion and Koda, at eight and six years old, are making their usual mess. On autopilot I remind them to be "careful of the chairs," but they only spin faster until Koda knocks into his sister and spills his water all over the counter and floor. I feel the day starting to spiral away, already. "Time to go outside!" I announce (more a demand), but Koda, always the homebody, refuses: "I can't, my boots feel funny on the snow." This is a new one.

After some back and forth to ascertain the logic behind this, I start losing patience, and as I am about to order him outside, Shakil catches the parenting ball and changes tactics: "I have a story for you." The kids loll back in their swivel chairs, wondering if this is a *real* story or a story dressed up as a lecture. "When I was in grade two, three years after we moved to Canada, I went to go skating one day. Dadu and Dado [grandfather and grandmother] didn't skate, and my sisters were too little, so I had to go on my own." The kids are now enraptured. They love stories of the past, our past. He continues, "While I was skating, the snow picked up, and it started to blizzard harder and harder. I went to sit down on the bench to unlace my skates, but my fingers were too cold, and there was no one around to help. I had to walk the rest of the way home with one skate on. THAT sure felt like it was hard to walk on the snow."

He's telling it in a way that is meant to be humorous, but Arion, already so intuitive, immediately bursts into tears. "Daaaaaaddy," she sobs, "you were leeeeeeeeft a-a-a-lone by y-y-yourself, and there was nooooooo one there to h-e-e-e-lp you. That makes me so sad."

We all try at various points to placate her. Shakil explains why Dado and Dadu weren't available to go with him. Koda makes a face at her and asks why she's crying so much. I try and give context of our growing up, that it was different then because kids were left on their own more, and, especially, that as new immigrants our families didn't know all the rules for winter. "You're all making it worse!" she wails.

Twenty minutes later she's still sitting in the chair crying. I pick her up and carry her into the living room, cradling her on my lap. "Da-a-a-ddy was a-a-a-lone," she stutters and starts crying afresh. "And no one he-e-e-elped him." I start to speak, then stop myself. I get an image of a seven-year-old boy, about the same age as she is now, sitting alone on a bench in the cold, fingers shaking, trying to undo his laces, and then slowly limping home through the whirling snow. The whole experience of immigration is right there ... the discomfort of a new environment, the challenging weather conditions, the isolation, always the isolation. I feel tears coming and pull my daughter's body more tightly into mine. Her emotions have opened a portal to the past, and now she's brought me there as well.

Shakil comes over and wisely suggests, "Why don't we play it out? I can sit here" — he gestures to the couch — "trying to unlace my skate and maybe you can come over and help me." She looks up at him and thinks it over. "You can use your kindness superpowers," he adds.

"Okay," she acquiesces.

He sits and fumbles around near his feet. She gingerly walks over and kneels down on the ground before him. "Can I help you?" she asks. My husband, age fifty-two or maybe seven again, just nods his head silently.

She pulls off his slipper. "Here you go!" she announces. "And do you need help walking home?"

"Yes," my husband simply says, and she takes his hand securely in her own.

After they walk a few steps, she lets go and spins around, dancing up the stairs to her next activity.

Later than morning, Shakil remarks how surprised he was at the feelings that emerged as they role-played the scenario. "What do you mean?" I ask.

"Well," and he pauses to think, "it was like something was completed. Like a part of me waiting for help was comforted, even though it's decades later and I hardly remember the incident."

❋

It's the Family Day holiday, so that afternoon we bundle ourselves into snowsuits to go on a nature walk nearby, in the ravine. After a half-hour of wandering over train tracks, feeding bread crumbs to a group of wild ducks, and stopping for snacks under snow-laden branches, we emerge through the trees, blinking in amazement. In front of us is a winter wonderland, bright clothing flashing in front of us in a kaleidoscopic blur. A small pond has been turned into a makeshift ice rink. Kids and adults are skating by with shovels to clear the snow. A motley crew of other folks are scattered around, eating, laughing, or helping little ones with their skates and snacks.

This scene has everything the other did not.

I look over at Shakil, awed at this magic we've stumbled upon. I think how that little boy is not alone anymore, and maybe he never was. Perhaps there were people hidden in that blizzard, out of sight, just around the corner. Isn't this what faith is? Trust that even when we're alone, there are people holding us from afar — like the people we're surrounded by, like a far and distant daughter? I look at our daughter now, with her hand in her father's, and feel past seeds sprouting toward wholeness. I offer silent gratitude for these unexpected invitations to unpack the years off our back, so we may settle more fully into the present and call it home.

5

SKY DANCING

It's not the weather I was hoping for. The sky has served up the usual fall order of tasteless grey on grey, a bland backdrop for our hurried steps. It's mid-November in Toronto, and my seven-year-old daughter, Arion, and I side-hop down the slippery stairs of the subway station, holding hands, arriving at the last moment to watch the train disappear. I manoeuvre her behind me as we move along the platform, weaving between suitcase-carrying professionals, headphone-wearing students, and other parents doing the post-school pick up.

"When's it coming?" she shrieks, causing heads to turn in our direction.

"One more minute," I assure her, hoping the next train is on time. As it comes crashing toward us, I caution her to step from solid platform on to machine in motion, making sure she doesn't fall through the gap. I think resignedly how deeply familiar I am to this practice as a first-generation immigrant.

All at once, the usual sensory landscape that accompanies a trip on the subway hits me. I first notice the faint scent of urine and floral perfume, then catch sight of a poster with the caption "Pigs Have Feelings Too." This is such a white person issue, I think, even as I commiserate with the pigs. So many efforts protecting animals that most Brown people don't touch, swine discrimination taking visible priority over the more ubiquitous human form.

My attention is pulled away by Arion jumping like an amphetamine-dosed rabbit across the rocking train floor. The person next to me, a young woman with a serious visage, stands up to offer my daughter her seat, her sudden bright smile like the sun coming out against this cloudy backdrop of sagging post-work slackness.

I interject hastily. "No, that's okay. She's happy to stand. Needs to work off some of that energy anyway!" My daughter beams at both of us as she twists away, and I admonish her to hold on to the pole, impressed as usual by her energy. She moves to the opposite side of the carriage to peer at the pig poster, and I am left holding the tatters of my own authority, experiencing habitual doubt about my parenting abilities.

As I look out the window, my reflection flickering in and out, I see *her*, my own seven-year-old self on a bus in downtown Tehran. "Stand up," my father's voice orders as he grabs my hand to offer my seat up to a face I didn't know then and can't remember now, installing the moral code of always deferring to elders. I'm always somewhat amazed, a generation later, to witness people of all ages stand and offer their seat to my daughter. I find myself frequently refusing even as she turns on the charm with a self-satisfied, "Thank you!" I don't want her to lose this concern, this invisible cultural glue of generosity toward strangers that is so much a part of Middle Eastern culture. I worry, *What else of my background, culture, and upbringing will be lost in this transfer of first-to-second-generation immigrant?*

I try and entice her over with a snack my parents would not have been able to afford: a chocolate-banana granola bar that is organic, vegan, and gluten free! She barely glances at it before declaring in a chastising tone, "I don't like this kind." I wonder what gifts she will keep, the kinds I wasn't able to carry with me through the years. She is pure exuberance, befriending all around us with her boundless curiosity and penetrating gaze. She was like this from the moment of birth, coming into the world all "Where's the party and how do I join?" before she chomped down hard on my breast like she was going to show me how it was done.

Arion makes up her own rules, never forgets a lyric to a song she's heard once, and can disappear for hours into her own imaginary worlds. Hubby often teases me: "What's it like to parent yourself?" Sometimes I laugh, other times I huff in frustration. Having a child with your temperament ups the parenting stakes, reflects more clearly both strengths, such as the ability to make up stories on the spot, but also weaknesses, like how quickly I resort to anger when repeating something for the seventh time. In such moments I want to blame my dad.

When I was a child, Dad was a typical father from a time period and a country where men were raised to be hard and proud. This led to his success in Iran but did not transplant well when we moved to a small city in Canada. He was never promoted beyond his entry level position regardless of how hard he worked, was often shunned at social events, and he, like me, was called "Paki" in public. His pride in the face of all this racism composted into rage, and as the eldest I took the brunt of it. I learned to brace in anticipation of his anger to protect the others in our family. I always knew he loved me; it was just that the stigma he faced turned into increased policing of my siblings and me, a perversion of the usual parental desire to protect.

This was part of the price of immigration, this dark, thick love woven inextricably with shame. One summer I showed him a pair of lopsided shorts I'd sewn in grade 7 home economics class that year. I was so proud of what I'd accomplished, this new ability to transform one thing into another. Yet he tore into me: "Get them off! They are so ugly. You should be pretty!" His mouth was twisted in scorn while his eyes pleaded with me to understand what he was really trying to convey: he didn't want me to fall short of the ideal image of the perfect girl (white, skinny, and impeccably dressed) as insurance against discrimination — toward both of us. I learned that I had to shape myself in ways that would make him proud. I cut a hole in the ceiling of my life and stuffed away all that marked me as Brown, Iranian, *different*.

I don't want my daughter to be haunted by the same identity ghosts as I was.

Arion's voice, a few decibels above usual conversation levels despite being right beside me, slams the memory vault shut. "I can't wait, Mama!" she proclaims as she hops up and down, already a black belt in the subway art of balancing on her feet. "I'm so glad we are *finally* on our adventure!"

I look around the carriage at the various bent heads, bright bags, and colourful posters, feel the gentle clanking under our feet, and finally turn to gaze into my daughter's joyous, upturned face. Her energy is infectious. I smile back at her, genuinely grateful as well to be on this adventure together.

We jump off and switch trains to the North-South line and a few minutes later speed into Union Station. Arion pulls me onto the waiting platform, and we make our way up the crowded stairs to finally breathe fresh air. This is a date I've promised now for over a year — to take her to the highest point in the city, once the highest structure in the world: the CN Tower, a place we see every day but have never visited. It's 553 metres tall, has 1,776 stairs, and is 113 stories stacked straight up in a gravity-defying structural invention, like a giant needle rising out of the ground with a doughnut on top — it's what people who aren't from Toronto think of when they visualize the city.

Despite its iconic status, it's a landmark of little beauty, with mostly sparse functionality. In the city, we like to wax rhetorically about its uniqueness, but it seems like male-driven capitalism at its best (or worst), a product of the seventies when white men and their money blatantly ruled the world. We share the same birth year of 1973, two years after the official policy of multiculturalism or "come hither, all immigrants" came into effect. Still, I wish we were known for something more aesthetically pleasing, like the Eiffel Tower, or the Statue of Liberty — the beauty of each softening the commanding presence of their height — but the CN Tower is familiar. It's the image I scan for in the skyline each time I fly back from away, reassuring me that, yes, I've landed in the right place.

We walk through the turnstiles and I offer my purse to security (another remnant of 9/11): two Brown guys in their mid-thirties, whose conversation I feel like we've interrupted. Arion thrusts her blue-grey, sparkly unicorn purse over the counter toward them, and I stifle a smile as I watch one of them gingerly pick it up by its purse strap, careful to avoid the protruding gilded horn. On autopilot, they rifle around inside, handing it back to me with a quick quirk of lips. *Good luck*, I imagine them thinking.

The elevator shoots us into the sky as we listen to the pock-faced boy in front of us recite his list of facts in staccato fashion, like how high we are going and at what death-defying speed. I spend most of the minute-long ride peeking down through the glass bottom of the elevator. Eventually, I have to look away, dizzy at how rapidly the ground is disappearing below us.

We step into the rounded corridor that hugs the inner spine of the tower. In the form of a series of elevators, this column carries people up and down, all day long.

I notice we are surrounded by a slice of the city; some people look like tourists and others like residents staycationing. I love this about Toronto: that people use our city well, visit its many festivals, neighbourhoods, and landmarks, and take pride in things that distinguish us. I notice a young white couple in their early twenties, the boy taking the girl's hand in a sweet gesture of proprietary affection. Beside them, a multigenerational Asian family of parents and two girls about the same age as mine, with shrunken grandparents in tow. Behind us, a group of thirtysomething women chattering like excited magpies, every skin tone represented in their small flock. One of them has on a bright orange silky scarf and it brushes my cheek momentarily, the gentle caress of a butterfly wing.

I feel my body relax in the presence of so many visible differences; my own blend into the surroundings and I'm freed from feeling self-conscious. This reality is light years away from the prairie suburb that surrounded my younger self, where our immigrant family always stood out, where second glances became second nature.

Arion tugs me forward. "This way, Mama!" I take her hand and let her lead us through the throngs of people. There are multiple café counters set up around us, eager to profit from the landmark. Each one carries many food options, as well as alcohol with specialized tourist shot glasses, and is staffed by Brown and Black folks of every ethnicity. Wanting something more substantial, we climb up a flight of stairs to the upscale restaurant that sits in the largest part of the tower to see a much whiter-washed, more sparsely populated human landscape.

While my daughter stands beside me, I ask to see a menu. I'm aware I'm wearing my usual cloak of friendliness, the immigrant hangover of wanting to please, layered over my quick-to-defend response underneath, knit together from the time I was Arion's age. The middle-aged white woman is hesitant to approach us. I expect she doesn't have many solo Brown women up here as customers. It is easier for her to assume disdain. I immediately know I won't eat here because of her, but I make a show of reading the menu, the obstinate impulse to defend myself, to prove my belonging in this space, now on high gear.

"Do you want to be seated?" she slowly asks, impatience lacing her tone. Without my awareness, Arion has wandered a few steps into the empty space. She follows it up by snapping, "Your daughter should not be going there!"

"No thanks," I slowly respond to her first question. Then I can't help remonstrating, my inner seven-year-old taking over. "There is barely anyone here. Why is it such a big deal?" I stand in awkward silence for a couple of beats, waiting to see if she will challenge me, unwilling to cede the ground my adult body has gained in the last forty years.

This ability to take my own side instead of giving into her disapproval is a remnant from my father, one I now recognize as a blessing. In his accented, broken English, he would have bulldozed, then brushed her aside: "Don't worry about her! Just give us a table." Unlike him, I know I have easier entry to these places, but like him I know I am not always welcome. My daughter, she will likely not recognize much, if any, difference in treatment. This is the reality of being a first-generation immigrant wedged between parents who lost so much in their move here, and my child who takes it all for granted. Although I mostly feel grateful for this adopted country, moments like this overdraw the gratitude I've banked.

The woman chooses to avoid my gaze as Arion takes my hand, the fight leaving my body as we slowly trudge downstairs. She asks in a more subdued voice than usual, "Were you upset with that lady, Mama?"

I pause for a moment and then frankly respond, "A little bit. I think she could have been nicer to us."

I want the shame I was forced to swallow about who I was, who my family were, where we came from, to have served a purpose: to protect her future, the future of all those not considered "true" Canadians. I will not pretend all is fine as my parents did with me. I want my daughter to know that identity — the body we are born into and the choices we make about who we are — always determines our ease of movement through the world, and not to take belonging for granted until it becomes the birthright for all that it ought to be.

We return to one of the snack kiosks to buy a hot dog and fries, a still overpriced choice but much more financially and emotionally palatable for our adventure today. The man behind the counter, who I read as South Asian, nods at us in acknowledgement as he types in our order. Arion leads me to a table by a tall window, and I reach into my purse to pull out our worn Uno card deck. I carefully lay the cards across the table.

The same man eventually brings over the tray, asking me with accented curiosity, "Where are you from?" I contemplate answering with my usual immigrant solidarity response, "Iran," but instead I pause. I have spent years befriending the annexed parts of myself, welcoming those old ghosts to re-inhabit the various limbs of my body and parts of my psyche. I have walked slowly over hot coals of shame that manifested through an eating disorder, obsessive-compulsive behaviours, anxiety, and depression to reclaim the hand of that inner seven-year-old and allow her the freedom to be herself. That I am here in this country, sitting here now with my daughter, able to be here as an embodied adult, seems suddenly its own kind of miracle.

"Here. I'm from here," I finally respond.

As Arion bites into her hot dog, her cheeks bulging and mustard dripping out of a corner of her mouth, I'm reminded again of my earlier self, sitting in the backseat of our car in downtown Tehran fighting with younger siblings over *Sangaak* bread, stuffing as much as possible into my mouth just as Arion is right now. In those early years, pre-immigration, I grew up taking for granted that it was okay to be loud and bold, to be the centre of attention, secure in the knowledge I was part of a community. As I take a bite of my own hot dog, I, too, find myself wiping a yellow stain off my sleeve. I know if my father were here he would fit right in this chewing, dripping assembly line. We are all alike in this essential way, linked by an intrinsic boldness that has held up across continents, cultures, and ocean.

My daughter will perhaps never realize it, but it is a gift she has inherited and one I will fiercely protect against both the outside world and also my own occasional unintentional backlash. Parenting her is parenting backward, toward all earlier versions of myself but also beyond, to our ancestors, nurturing a cultural essence that has allowed us all to survive and thrive. Arion may not always defer to elders but she reflects the loud, passionate face of our culture. She will be Iranian in ways she might never realize, because of generations of people she'll never know. And in spite of — no, because of this audaciousness — I want her to grow up feeling entitled to stand as high, as tall, as unapologetic as this emblem of traditional power we are standing in.

We finish eating and finally make our way around the observation deck to visit the glass panels that line the floor of the tower, the main attraction. Most adults are tentatively hunched around the edges, peering over to see the ground over three hundred metres below. Even though it's several centimetres of fortified glass and the poster beside us says it can hold thirty-five moose, possibly the most stereotypically Canadian of measurements, it's against instinct to stand on something so seemingly fragile, requiring faith that the step beyond solid ground will hold. Arion starts skipping across the glass floor.

"Aren't you scared?" I ask.

Her body, full of exuberance, moving in rhythm to a nonsensical improvised tune sung loudly enough so all around can hear, is answer enough: "I'm dancing here at the CN Tower, just my mama and me. We came by train and had a snack, and now ... I have to pee!"

Seeing how she's managing just fine on her own, I eye the wall behind us, wondering if I can go sit down and close my eyes for a bit to limit the vertigo. Before I can move, my daughter interrupts, suddenly grabbing my hand to once again pull me along behind her. "Follow me, Mama," she says. "You just have to try it." Then she pauses and adds with emphasis, "But it's better if you dance!"

Taking a deep breath and surrendering caution, I grab her hands and swing her around, irrationally praying that the transparent glass under our feet will hold us up. It does.

"Yippee!" I hear myself call out.

Temporarily, we are goddesses caught between the heavens and the earth below, moving limbs in our own improvised creation dance. In many ways, this is the essence of immigration: a prayer flung across borders and generations trusting the unknown to hold you as well, or better, than what you leave behind.

As I spin with my girl, out of the corner of my eye I notice that at this height the grey sky has taken on a silver hue.

TRANSPLANT

Sometimes when I'm talking with my sister, tilling the soil of our shared memories of immigration and its aftermath, I'll sink into the dense dry darkness and remember how inhospitable this land was for us when we were abruptly uprooted and transplanted from afar.

I'll remember how little air or water there was and how long it took to grow roots.

I'll remember how sometimes we fought each other like weeds competing for the sun's light and warmth.

I'll feel envious of the roses, those tall, coveted blooms with their thorns that prick so easily yet are always forgiven their sharpness, unlike us thistles, resilient yet expendable.

Then I will remember that being a transplant means growing between what was before and what's to come.

That I will leave fertile soil behind in what was fallow ground.

That each new seed coming will be fed by what we shed.

THREADS

When I was ten, a year after we moved to Alberta from Iran, we went to visit some friends about an hour's drive away. The grandmother was a crocheter, and before we left, she handed me a single square of pastel pink, purple, and yellow hues (softer than my favourite vibrant colours). She suggested that "perhaps you could wash dishes with it." Instead, I slept with it curled in my right fist every night for the next five years.

This random gift from a woman I met only once became the object without which I couldn't sleep at night. Many a bedtime found my mother wrestling with sheets, engaged in some bizarre game of Twister while searching for the missing square, as I stood idly by giving (not so helpful) directions about where I'd seen it last.

At that point, I was hanging on by threads to who I was. Immigration, racism, and social shunning hammered away at the girl I had been in Tehran, reworking me into a pastel version of myself in this new land. In the midst of all this, I clutched at those crocheted threads for comfort in the terrifying dark. Often the generous loops mopped up my tears. Sometimes, as the square scraped against my childhood skin, it was a physical reminder that, yes, I was still visible. Alive.

Like many childhood loves, this cloth soother was discarded in the transition to adulthood. It is sitting in a box in my mother's house, forgotten but for its connection to the past — a collection of threads representing the fabric of my childhood. Yet its memory reminds me what belonging is, how simple it can be, that its possibility exists everywhere. And that sometimes it can come from a stranger's unexpected generosity, handing us the next thing that will help get us through.

SHOLEH ZARD

There is a Persian rice pudding the colour of an egg yolk, flavoured with saffron and rosewater and artfully topped with cinnamon and pistachios, that is served at festivals and celebrations. It's the perfect amount of sweetness and can be eaten for dinner or dessert. It tastes like the past — childhood condensed into a single bowl of sun.

My eight-year-old daughter, Arion, wants to do her first school report on *Sholeh Zard*, but though I can summon the flavour I am no expert in making it. I've eaten it at every Iranian family and cultural celebration I've attended but have never made it myself. With Google as a guide, she is able to painstakingly summarize the following key facts:

1. Ingredients include basmati rice, saffron, butter, sugar, rosewater, cardamom, nuts.
2. It takes about four hours to make.
3. It is a centuries-old recipe and used to be served only at *Nowrooz*, the Persian New Year.
4. You can make a wish while cooking that should it come true, you are indebted to give back by sharing the dish widely with strangers.
5. It is universally loved in Iran.

Naturally, it's not enough to record these facts, have a conversation with my father about it, or draw a detailed picture of *Sholeh Zard*, without also attempting to make it. We print out the recipe.

I buy rosewater and pistachios. Arion names the date, a nondescript Saturday morning.

The day of, I'm downstairs twisting tight muscles into various poses. Tired of the lack of exercise in this pandemic—second wave, I've signed up for a new online yoga class. A few minutes in, I hear Arion's voice wafting down from above barking out instructions to her father. I am not surprised she's unable to wait for me to begin.

I continue pushing through the motions, half focused on the culinary drama unfolding on the floor above me and half fighting off the exhaustion I feel. As I swing around into one of the familiar stances, my right shoulder dislocates. I cry out in pain. Shakil and Arion run downstairs as I brace, praying I can manage to lever the joint back into place.

It's my lucky day. Holding my right shoulder socket gingerly I lean over at the waist and force myself to slowly lift my right arm. I'm panicking but my daughter's presence at the door forces me into calm action. I sag in relief a minute later when I feel the upwards traction allow the joint to slip back into place, releasing me from the trauma of sitting with ever worsening pain for hours, waiting for morphine and medical intervention. Offering a silent prayer of thanks for avoiding a hospital trip this time, I gingerly lie on the bed, accept an ice pack and some Advil, and close my eyes to rest. I'm woken an hour later by a knock on the door, followed closely by Arion's piercing voice, "Mama, are you awake? I have something for you!"

"I am now," I murmur.

She carefully comes in, holding a tray with a glass of milk and some cookies. "What's that?" I ask. "I thought you were making *Sholeh Zard*!"

"It would take too long, and we didn't have the right rice to make it, so Daddy and me used the ingredients to make these instead."

"Ohhh," I manage to say, looking at the muddy-coloured, misshapen blobs on my plate. Instead of a yellow sun, there is a plate of turds before me. "Thank you." I have enough parenting years under my belt to know not to complain at what is being presented to me.

"Be careful of your shoulder, Mama. Here!" Arion picks up one of the shapes and shoves it into my mouth. Unprepared, I let crumbs fall on the bedspread as I hurriedly chew.

This is no *Sholeh Zard*. It's not creamy, nor is it yellow, nor is it rice based. It does not look appetizing. But with my daughter's eyes closely fixed on my face, I close my eyes to dutifully savour the mouthful.

My shoulders slowly lower a couple of inches. I focus on my chewing. Though it's not in the form I anticipated, I can still feel the distant echo of ancestors and the seductive power of rosewater. Culture is not merely passed on through language. It's transmitted primally through the body via tastes, smells, and sights that pull us back to a time where we took belonging for granted, where food was love. This *Sholeh Zard* doesn't have to be what I expected to offer the comfort I need. Old traditions can take on new forms and still be delicious. I decide we are a Brown blob family, and this is about as Persian as we're going to get. It's good enough for me.

Smiling at my daughter, I pick up another shape from the plate. She does the same. Together we silently munch away, connected through the culture exploding in our grateful mouths.

6

REBEL BODY

Blood

I t's early days in our business, and today I've upped my game for the group I'm presenting to — a hundred managers within a government ministry. I'm wearing a Kate Spade, above-the-knee, black wool skirt with a gold zipper in the back, a tucked-in white shirt, sheer black tights, and for the first time ever, a pair of high heels. Not just any high heels: I went all in and bought a pair of four-inch, black patent stilettos. Because they are new, I'm teetering slightly, belatedly realizing that to walk confidently in heels means holding the body differently: chest up, bum out. You need to stride confidently to pull these shoes off well. In the not-so-far-off future, I will be able to carry off this power strut (mostly, and only for confined chunks of time), but right now I'm like a newly hatched chick on ice.

After arriving, I start setting up at the front of the room. As I'm fiddling with the projector controls, I feel a slight trickle of wetness below. With minutes to spare before the session starts, I escape to the bathroom, walking as quickly as my spindly platforms will allow. Once inside the stall, I realize that my underwear, tights, and even thighs are covered in blood. *Fuuuuuuuck.* This used to happen when I was first getting my period, I think. Once, in grade 7, I made the mistake of wearing white jeans to school and ended up with a stain the size of Russia on my backside. It was an event not soon forgotten by my peers (nor, apparently, by me). Not expecting my flow today, and in my rush to arrive on time, I didn't bring any hygiene products with me. I'm forced to slowly teeter back into the room, retracing my steps to politely inquire of my client contact if she can track down something for me to use. Back in the same bathroom a few minutes later, I quickly wash as much red out of my garments as I can, afterward holding soggy panties and tights under the dryer, praying they won't be too wet, hoping there will be no odour.

I glance down at my beautiful new shoes, this societal status symbol I've chosen to embrace for events such as this. They don't seem so powerful now. I let out a long sigh, feeling the shame tornado start to swirl within. It doesn't matter how much I try to mould this body into modern beauty standards, she always pulls me back down to earth. Being in a non-white body isn't just about being treated differently because of features, body shape, or skin colour. Whiteness as a culture is built on what can be controlled, measured, and, ultimately, commodified. Racialized bodies colour out of these lines. Non-white bodies are considered unruly: we have bigger hair, hips, lips, and asses; loud voices, earth rhythms, and collectivist cultures that take up too much space, are too messy, too hard to predict. *Too, too, too …*

It's why so many people of colour coming from cultures like mine try and stuff themselves into white, Anglo-Saxon, Protestant (WASP) straitjackets to succeed. If our hair could be straighter, our bodies hairless, our thighs slimmer, our voices quieter, our manners accommodating, our heights taller, maybe then we'd be in the club. It's almost always less of something. The higher one climbs the ladder of success, the stronger the pressure to conform to these standards and the greater the penalty for not doing so. I wonder if my body is rebelling against the perfectionist pressure I put on myself in places like this, where I feel I can't have a hair or word out of place. We can deny our culture, homeland, people, and ancestors, but these powers course through our blood, manifest through temperament and personality. They speak most loudly through body symptoms when denied too long, when the gap between where we came from and where we are trying to fit in becomes unbearable. Perhaps this flow of red tears is here to remind me: "Fuck trying to change yourself. Power is in *here*, not in your heels."

Bile

I always knew my body was unruly — that it didn't fit the "good girl" ideal. After being forced from Iran at seven years old, I learned, first in England and then in Canada, to be suspicious of my body because it stood out from the other bodies around me. Copious and conspicuous amounts of hair when thick brows weren't in and sideburns were a liability, uncontrollable curls that stayed in a constant (square) mullet throughout the eighties, hips that wouldn't shrink, dark olive skin that no foundation or lipstick colour ever worked on, heavy bleeding that never seemed to flow easily or on schedule. There was also that hot-blooded Persian passion. Were strong feelings indicative of temperament or culture, personality or survival? Ultimately, it didn't matter; I fulfilled all the recycled Persian stereotypes of being loud, opinionated, exotic … and a little neurotic.

When I was eighteen years old, in my last year of high school, nine years after immigrating to Canada, obsessive-compulsive behaviours and insomnia could no longer contain the tsunami of my repressed feelings. The loss of everything that had been ripped away, the rage at the rejection we faced, the fear of being not normal, all engulfed me, and I turned to bingeing and purging food. I was applying to universities, feeling my worth and my family's sacrifice were on the line, and something had to give. Food was the most dependable crutch — it was always available, rarely noticeable, and easily dispensable; it was a *smart* addiction — allowing me to succeed publicly while coping in private, my body taking the brunt of what I couldn't risk expressing.

I went across the country to Queen's, the whitest university in the country, after high school. I went into business, the whitest faculty within the university (there were only two of us non-white bodies in the class of about a hundred). The first week of frosh parties illuminated a world I wasn't aware existed. On a houseboat one night, red plastic cup in hand with some electric blue substance sloshing about within, wind whipping my still badly cut hair across my cheeks, I overheard a couple of classmates talking. "My dad called the chair and gave a donation. I didn't make the list at first ..." and the reply, "Ha ha ha, you should talk to John over there! Same story ..." I felt like I was on another planet, with blond, blue-eyed people speaking a language foreign to me. Family connections. Old money. Nepotism. I don't know what I was thinking going to that university, though in retrospect rationality didn't drive the decision much at all. Stress and addiction had forced me onto the path of pleasing others (namely my father) and so I went, believing it was the best path to personal and familial redemption.

I chose perhaps the most unfriendly academic environment in the country for someone like me — a nerdy, sensitive, artistic soul — who, more than anything, wanted acceptance. I couldn't imagine that some twenty years later I would be in front of folks of this ilk, not as a colleague but as someone brought in to speak, teach, and improve unfair and discriminatory cultures. It would have shocked my younger self to know how many of these peers would cling stubbornly to their belief in meritocracy: the idea that they got into top leadership roles because of their innate talent and skill as opposed to the unearned privilege of their white skin, rich families, and network of connections. These inner circles of race, money, and historical power run our country — and most countries — to this day. Yet we still entertain the myth that racial inequality is about inferiority rather than just plain old unfairness. Starting my adult journey away from home in such a place only cemented my self-abusive behaviour.

Over the next decade, I dealt with the fear of not meeting white people's standards by stuffing endlessly white substances — bread, cake, ice cream, rice — down my throat, maybe in hopes of eventually becoming white enough from the inside out to pass. But then I'd always follow such sessions by sticking a fork down my throat and forcing myself to throw it all up, the decision to rebel in this way giving back a temporary feeling of power. Forcing myself to throw up food and nourishment felt like a regaining of control in a culture and country where I often felt I had little control in my body and identity. Purging the stockpiles of shame — the feeling that *I* was the problem, not the systems I was caged by — offered a temporary but satisfying feeling I was truly in charge of my destiny. Each rush of food forced from out of my throat felt like a roaring of unspoken words I didn't know how to say in other ways.

I left Queen's University after the first year, returning to western roots that, if not more welcoming, were, at least, familiar. I moved near campus at the University of Alberta and found a few friends who stuck. I got elected to the Academic Governors' Council, worked for the Students' Union, got good grades. After graduating, I volunteered for a provincial political campaign and started working in the Alberta Legislature Building, in Edmonton. I was noticed for my work and soon moved to Ottawa, our nation's capital, to lead a couple of cross-country campaigns focused on planetary justice. I met with politicians and media, thought leaders, and lobbyists. Outwardly I was on fire, inwardly I was struggling.

Then a plane hit a New York City tower. The world as we knew it instantly changed, and the public and private parts of myself could no longer be held apart: I was of Middle Eastern descent and part of a group painted as the global threat, I was the child on TV bullied because of my identity, I was the activist labelled as terrorist. The scab over the trauma I had accumulated and suppressed since that first moment of immigration was ripped off. Raw and wild emotions gushed to the surface. I was almost thirty years old and felt like one big, pulsing, open wound. The only way I knew how to deal was by bingeing and purging multiple times a day. My body was screaming loudly, but I had no idea how to get in touch with the hidden story.

Looking for the quickest escape route, and knowing I had to tend to internal injuries, I dove into the world of eastern spirituality, yoga, and mindfulness meditation. I applied and was accepted into a months-long spiritual lifestyle program at a major U.S. retreat centre. Slowly, as I learned to connect with what I was feeling, the desire to vomit out all my emotions gradually diminished. I started to understand there was more to my story than what I was able to do or accomplish. There were parts of my story I was not allowing myself to see. I began to understand there would be risks associated with allowing myself to see the whole story rather than just the parts that conveniently fit with our cultural myth of benevolent acceptance of outsiders. Because there was no story where I saw myself reflected, I had to write my own. The process began in earnest when I started to tune in and slowly digest the past, allowing me to see the present more and more clearly.

Bone

It was around the time the bulimia started, in my last year of high school, that my bones started to speak.

To lose the weight I'd gained from over-studying and under-exercising, I decided to join our high school's inaugural girls' rugby team. This was the late eighties, when girls playing traditionally male sports was still newsworthy. We had a couple months of practice before the big first game. Both my parents came out to watch. Each time our white German coach blew his whistle, yelling, "Move, move!" I obediently ran as fast as I could. My right shoulder got hit hard. There was no break so I kept moving. At a certain point, I lost momentum but didn't feel I could stop. Again, my shoulder took someone's elbow. I knew this wasn't a space where weakness would be understood; here it would, in fact, be a character flaw. It was just after halftime when another body slammed into mine, finally knocking the right shoulder bone out of joint. As I was loaded into the ambulance, the game behind me kept on going.

I could hear the cheers and the faint cries of my coach as my body was loaded onto the gurney. That night I spent hours in the hospital, introduced to morphine for the first time as my shoulder was wrenched back into place. No one, not my coach nor any member of the team, called to see how I was doing — not that evening, nor after I'd missed the next couple of practices. And when I attended a practice, arm in sling, so I could fill my coach in on the prognosis, I was met with "That's not true! Your arm didn't dislocate. I've seen that happen to players and it wasn't what happened to you!" The injury was bad enough, but the denial of the injury was worse. I was being gaslit over something doctors had diagnosed. I swallowed it though, because believing in others' version of reality over my own was how I survived.

Every year for the next twenty years, my shoulders repeatedly dislocated. The bones easily slid out of place when coughing or reaching over to pick up a glass of water from the bedside table. These moments, inevitably requiring repeat hospital visits, were beams falling onto a crumbling internal foundation. I was a high achiever, so I could always perform. What I couldn't do was manage the backstage of my life. I frequently felt overwhelmed. I found it hard to stay balanced in intimate relationships. I continued to struggle with anxiety, depression, and obsessive behaviour. But these words look so neat and ordered on a page. To capture the desperation, the journey of more than five thousand nights and days searching for something that I didn't know how to name, trapped in a body that repeatedly threw out its guts to get past the panic over small slights that might finally expose me as a fraud, is impossible. I felt like I was on an island, inside a cage of bones I did not know how to break out of. My body did the next closest thing — occasionally sliding open the door of the cage, taking bones out of joint, reminding me there was a way out.

Our deepest maps — paths to who we are and what we are meant to be doing — are coded in the bone. Bones are what we leave behind when we die — this skeleton not of our choosing, but which becomes indelibly ours through living. Bones are witness to every experience. So deeply buried, they are often immune to attempts of transformation or beautification; by early adulthood ossification is complete. Bones are corporeal truth tellers of who we are, where we have come from, and, if we can listen, where we need to go. It took me until mid-life, more than two decades later, to finally listen to what my bones were telling me.

After another dislocation and hospital visit when I was around forty years of age, I mentally threw my hands up. I'd recovered a mostly good relationship with food. I took time to (mostly) feel my emotions. Yet, I felt helpless and didn't know what was missing. Being a new parent, I had a lot more time on my hands, away from the grind of work and focused on our mutual survival, to think.

Taking the time to mentally unravel the threads of my past, I decided it might help to go back to the first community I'd landed in in Canada — the elementary school I'd started at in grade 3. I had to wait until I returned home on a cross-country trip, and by this time, I'd built up anticipation of the visit. Yet, as I passed through the quiet hallways in my adult body, catching sight of my nine-year-old face in an old set of black-and-white photographs, I could slowly feel all energy drain from my body. Walking past the office, I went in to see if the same principal was there as when I attended. The administrator, an older, ash blond, apple-cheeked white woman curtly replied that he had left two years prior.

Suddenly desperate for validation, unsure of what to expect, I continued, "I went to this school after immigrating here. There was a lot of racism and bullying … at that time." To make clear the impact, I added, "It's taken me years to digest what happened." I waited for her to say something as the moment stretched awkwardly. Finally, she looked up and snapped, "I can't help you. And you shouldn't be in the school without permission." She lowered her gaze, signalling the conversation was over. It was like being stuck in a long camera shot in a key scene from my own life movie, except I couldn't remember my next lines. As I stared down at her polished hair, it dawned on me how familiar this felt. The moment was a microcosm of attempts to name racism with white people: deny, dismiss, minimize, or ignore.

It struck me that "in the school without permission" translated into feeling unable to be myself without the acknowledgement, validation, or approval of the white people around me who couldn't or wouldn't accept the ways my race, culture, and personality did not fit into their norms. And "I can't help you" pretty much said it all. The only tweak I would have made to the script is replacing "can't" with "won't." What people fail to realize is that belonging is not about accepting people who are like you; it's about working to see and accept people as they are, especially the ways they're different from you. It's seeing the patterns in who is being ritually left out or treated unfairly. Ultimately, it's about extending empathy, believing that someone else's experience of reality can indeed be different than yours. The administrator's words were a tipping point. Sitting outside the doors of the office, I thought I could finally see the story. The trauma of being treated as inferior, ugly, shameful had nothing to do with me. If she couldn't see this gorgeous creature in front of her now, how could the people here then possibly have seen the me of thirty years prior?

All change starts with naming. A correct diagnosis ensures the right medicine. Seeing the rejection in the context of racial trauma was incredibly healing because it validated all the symptoms my body developed to call my attention inwards. My coping patterns of overworking started to make sense. I began to understand seemingly separate patterns of isolation and withdrawal coupled with intensity and overwhelm, and I wrote about them in my first book, *Breaking the Ocean*. The waves of emotions that came out through an eating disorder, migraines, hair loss, and multiple dislocations all came together as I knit memories with spools of words. The story garment in the form of my memoir was gorgeous. I wrapped it around me as I walked out into the world.

My bones did not dislocate after the naming. Writing my story saved me.

Story

The story that is *ours*, the one that is most deeply nourishing, the one that will lead us forward, courses through blood, is digested or eliminated through bile, and lives in the bone. But living the story, knowing the story, and then speaking the story are all different stages of growth. Our bodies are wise. If we feel the story will not be heard or will get us pushed out of the group or away from success, many of us hold the story back. But the body always calls us back to our original home. It turns out that speaking my story was my final bridge to cross.

Soon after finishing writing my story in the form of a memoir, I travelled two hours outside Toronto, to a smaller, whiter city, to be part of a trauma training program. I wasn't surprised to see that most of the fiftyish participants in the room were casually dressed white women (think variations on Meryl Streep through the years). Toward the end of one of the training sessions, I volunteered to go up to the front of the room and be a guinea pig. Trauma training is aptly named because the training itself does indeed bring up one's unprocessed ... trauma. As soon as I was in front of everyone, performance anxiety kicked in. Guided to notice how my body was feeling, I immediately felt a wave of heat and slowly started to curl my head down into my chest — a classic posture of deferment, maybe shame. The trembling words that leaped from my mouth to finally run free in the silent room surprised me. "I felt so unsafe in rooms like this, full of white people who *never* understood." It was a new moment to name this so personally, in front of so many people. I allowed myself to curl the rest of the way over until my head was in my lap. I held back my tears. It took me awhile to integrate back into the shape of my adult self. Strength is measured by vulnerability, and I was proud of the risk I'd taken to give words to body experience in such a raw way.

The next day, our last day of training, I went out for lunch with another participant before heading out early to make the drive back to Toronto. She wanted to talk to me about equity and inclusion issues. Toward the end of our meal, she leaned forward, catching me off guard. "But it must be hard to deal with people's judgments, right?"

"What do you mean?" I asked.

"After you did your session with the instructor in front of everyone, one of the women in our group said, 'Why is she talking about white people like that? She's being racist. Who is she anyway?' None of us knew how to respond." I looked at her in shock, wondering why she was sharing this with me. She continued, oblivious. "What should I have said?"

It felt like being kicked in the centre of an old wound that I'd just picked the scab off of. This became another moment echoing the million moments where it wasn't safe to be who I am. I finished lunch post-haste, speed-walked back to my car, and started the engine. I was boiling inside, feeling both nauseous and furious, vulnerable and enraged at the same time. I decided this was not a moment I wanted to swallow and then have to deal later with a four-day migraine. Without thought, I walked back to the building, up the stairs, and into the room where the session had started up again. The words marched out of my belly this time: "Excuse me! I'd like to address something I just heard ... and I want you to imagine a woman speaking about her gender trauma a generation ago in front of a room of men. Imagine what their dismissal would have felt like! I should not have to deal with this."

I found myself then in the not unusual situation of having to educate and facilitate people's varying reactions to my truth-speaking. The instructor didn't say anything. One of the assistants said, "We all say things we don't mean," and I wondered how she interpreted that the comments were unintentional. After a few minutes of this, I politely thanked the group and walked out. I didn't return for the next session, or ever. But as I was driving back, once the stun effect had worn off, I started to laugh. What trauma takes away from people is voice, their *story*. Apparently, I had to attend trauma training to fully test out and reclaim my own. This time I was able to lean into unruliness and it felt like the best kind of power. I opened the window, turned the music up, and sang my lungs out the rest of the way home.

Two months later, I saw the instructor's name on the registration for our next inclusion training. And a year later, that same instructor brought Anima Leadership in to do an inclusion training for their global faculty team. Learning to be in my own skin took a lifetime of unlearning what I had needed to learn to survive immigration and immersion into white society. When I speak now, I know people will listen.

Finding belonging in the body is a beautiful struggle. It is nothing short of revolutionary because the language of the body helps us connect to the truest story, the story that will set us free. For a long time I couldn't access steadfast confidence or power because I didn't know how to place myself anywhere. But when I could see myself as the heroine of my own story, I could rescue myself and approach the castle that had always been out of reach. I was finally able to sit on the throne at the centre of my own life. The more of us that can see and reclaim the truth of our journeys and feed this back into the world, the greater our chance of changing the future of our collective story on this glorious planetary body we inhabit together.

BEAUTY

I'm lying on my back, trying not to scrunch up my face in response to the zaps of pain travelling across my arm like tiny drill bits digging past the barrier of skin. "Ouch!" I call out as the heat comes closer, goes deeper. "Mmmm," I hear in lukewarm acknowledgement. After it's over, I notice a hole burned through my new green cotton shirt. "Put on more aloe vera gel when you get home. Try not to go into the sun too much." Though it's August and twenty-five degrees Celsius outside. "And call us if your skin gets *really* red. Otherwise, see you in two weeks!" the aesthetician chirps.

I walk out in a daze, wondering why I continue to subject myself to this — laser hair removal. In the name of what: beauty? Beauty standards, the universal oppressor. How much we are pressured to do, how much we choose to do, and how much we do to each other in her name. What am I to say when my daughter gets older and complains of body hair? At nine years old, I can already see her Persian genes have won this genetic arm wrestle. I want to be principled and remind her: "Sweetheart, no one should have to change themselves to fit in," but I also *want* her to fit in for her own emotional health. Belonging always asks us to make a choice between freedom and conformity. Either way there's a cost.

Choosing to just let ourselves *be* means swallowing others' judgment and, usually, ongoing rejection. I remember in high school being desperate for any excuse to turn around and face my classroom crush. In my dreams we would talk and laugh, *connect*. In reality, I'd find him staring, in barely disguised disgust, at my arm covered in its mass of dark hair. I longed for the delicate, pale long limbs ascribed to every major female heroine we read about: Madame Bovary, Anna Karenina, Tess of the d'Urbervilles, Blanche DuBois, Nora Helmer, Cleopatra, and so on (and on and on and on). Do I tell my daughter to leave the hair, load on the makeup, and pose photos of herself on Instagram? Will that be enough, what, *insurance*, against the millions of moments in the real world where people will glance, look away, glance, look away, as they did in response to me? Is rejecting dominant beauty norms worth facing social judgment?

But even in conforming, there's a different price to pay. The majority of Persian women of a certain class get nose jobs. Many under-eighteen East Asian girls are known to get eyelid surgery. In most Brown- and Black-dominant countries, skin bleaching products are the highest sellers as women try to lighten and whiten their skin tone. Aging women are flocking in record numbers to get Botox and plastic surgery. Feminism today gives permission to choose to do whatever we wish to our bodies as long as it makes us feel more powerful, though as I leave the clinic after this laser treatment, I feel anything but. I'm kind of dizzy, my body numb from thirty minutes of ... well, discomfort and pain. It hits me that I have to dissociate from my body in order to improve it. My mind is the colonizer, my body the colonized. This does not fit my vision of liberation, where I live each day with mind, body, and spirit in healthy alignment.

Beauty is a close relative of belonging. If you're considered beautiful, your belonging is guaranteed in every room you enter. It doesn't mean being *liked*, but it does mean no one questions your right to be there and take up space. No wonder we spend so much time, effort, and money trying to acquire more beauty. It's the most powerful currency of all for buying ourselves universal access to social acceptance. But if we get it, do we actually feel like ourselves any longer?

I didn't go back to the clinic after that treatment. I had lasered half the hair off my arms, and I like the ones that are left. I wouldn't feel like me if they all disappear. I've drawn my line at the surface of my skin. Makeup, shaving, waxing, piercing: okay. Injecting myself, plastic surgery, anything that means plumbing, drilling, or mining this body I am in relationship with feels ... oppressive. I know my body is keeping the score. Our bodies are all keeping the score.

We all need to find our own relationship to belonging: What are we willing to change about ourselves to conform to modern (read: white and Western) beauty standards, and what do we hold on to because this or that feature comes down from ancestral lines, many of which are going extinct? My body hair, my larger than average nose mark me indelibly as from the Middle East, Iran, as do the shape of my eyes and long lashes. They define me as belonging to a particular group of people with whom I share a gene pool. When I remember this, I *feel* powerful rather than imagining the feeling of power, and this time it's a lion's roar pulsing beneath my skin, roaring across generations for the right to exist.

Beauty defined through our diversity is the rarest and most precious kind. Perhaps the most painful truth is that I have spent most of this life hating and hurting the parts of me that are *different*, wishing I was in a better — slimmer, taller, lighter, hairless — body. This is true for so many of us. The beauty industry globally is a booming multibillion-dollar marketplace thriving on the need for continuous self-improvement. Yes, choosing to pose and post on social media can be liberating, but it also reinforces the deadly notion that our self-worth is connected to how we look. It's a toss-up which way it'll go for my daughter's generation. I hope I pass on to her the courage to live as she is in her own skin, to actually let that lion's roar out of every pore, to love herself so deeply the world can't take her worth away, and she doesn't need to prove it to anyone. That kind of love, that's going to be the most beautiful revolution of all.

TOUCH

"You look old," my eight-year-old daughter says to me. "You *are* old."

"Not so much," I respond, rather affronted as I've not yet passed over the threshold of fifty, the official marker of middle age. "Some people think I'm still in my thirties." Although as I say this, I can't recall the last time this happened.

"Okay," she agrees, "but your *hands* look old."

I stare down at these hands I have a hard time keeping supple, a certain stiffness entering at times, early signs of arthritis, perhaps. These hands that washed my grandmother's body after death, which massage my mother's shoulders and hold my husband's waist before sleep. These hands I use to soothingly hug my body while in shades of distress and to gently wash my face each morning and night. These hands that have waved signs and changed diapers, typed out books, and wiped down floors. Hands that have touched thousands of people and held close those I have loved. These hands that hold my life while acting as a lifeline.

"They might look old, Arion," I retort, "but they have a lot of living left in them."

I glance her way, wondering how much I will be able to pass on to her, how long I have to do so. I see her future self walking the streets of a foreign city, hand in hand with a stranger. In my mind's eye, her head is down as she's madly typing to tame the wildness of her words; she's onstage holding a microphone as she pours the enormity of her voice into it; she's baking away as she loves to do. I wonder if she will be near when I pass and if she, too, will wash my body down with her hands, bidding me a silent farewell. I can't see her yet holding a child of her own. Perhaps we both need to be older for that.

As we walk on, I share nothing of these thoughts that I realize are uniquely tied to this passage of mid-life, knowing they will evoke only another "Mommy, you're weird" if said out loud. I simply and silently reach for her hand, hoping she will remember how mine feels instead of how it looks. My hands may look old but they are strong, and I squeeze her fingers tightly, hoping she will absorb some of this resilience through our fragile touch, that she will remember my grip when I am gone.

GROWN-UP

It's the morning of my forty-fifth birthday, unremarkable really, except that another 365 days, or 8,760 hours, have whizzed by. I get dressed carefully to drop off my five-year-old daughter to daycare, choosing an ankle-length embroidered red dress and fire-engine lipstick to match. If we age right, maybe we gain wisdom while shedding some of that ingrained self-inhibition.

"Why are you all dressed up, Arion's mom?" The other children cluster around when we arrive, their shrill voices cutting through the protective layers of memory until they reach the girl buried inside.

"Because it's my birthday today," I explain proudly.

They nod wisely, ten bright balls bobbing in tandem.

I wonder if I've got it wrong. Maybe we come in with wisdom, and growing up is nothing more than a journey to get back to where we started. I hold my head higher, as the girl within proudly basks in their unconditional approval.

7

FOREIGN OBJECT

Beware of telling the truest story.
How do you know which one is true?
The words will come from bone and burn you in the
  telling.
Freedom always comes at a cost.

I stand at the counter watching steam rise as water descends over the jagged bits of ginger below. The mug is too hot to hold, so I wrap my fingers around the handle and carry it over to our grey couch. As I lower myself into the cushiony softness, I feel a yawn clawing up my chest into my throat. My first book, a memoir, has just been released, and I feel like I've finally finished a long trek up the mountain. While proud to have arrived, I'm also exposed to all the elements and finding it hard to breathe. Suddenly I hear cries of what must be a wild animal, only to quickly realize it's my own voice, harsh and primal. I feel something trapped deep in my right upper leg and vagina, a bear's fangs sunk deep into layers of skin. There is nowhere to escape the aftermath of boiling water.

"Are you sure you still want to travel tomorrow?" Shakil asks, after time has passed. He's done his best to support me as I sit doubled over at the dining table, tears dripping into silence. I survey the enormity of the trembling raw skin now covering most of my upper thighs.

"No choice." I grind out the words. "More pills. And the other ice pack."

The next day I am embarking on two months of almost continuous travel to twelve North American cities, with sometimes two or more events per day, for *Breaking the Ocean*, my story about integrating the lifelong impacts of exile, immigration, racism, and trauma. The book is a corporeal cartography. I have written about obsessive-compulsive behaviour and bulimia, debilitating migraines and chronic depression. When I was in the writing process I thought I was ready to revisit the past and speak about it, but I never imagined journeying like this. Wounded, a foreigner once again in the landscape of my own skin. I didn't yet realize that telling the story meant the courage to relive it. I've since learned this is often how healing occurs: present-day injuries triggering echoes of past hurts, an unasked for, often unwelcome, do-over.

One of the first destinations is to our capital city, Ottawa, a place I once briefly lived in my mid-twenties. I have been invited to speak at an event (unpaid) at the National Gallery of Canada on the topic of "living well." I am supposed to feel honoured (which I am) while trying not to count the hours it took me to prepare and rehearse this talk amid the precious time spent juggling my clients, children, and house before departure. I deliver a speech covering systemic racism and its manifestations in front of a packed auditorium of hundreds of anonymous faces. The topic is about belonging and how often it's the small things that undermine our feeling of being welcomed, micro-exclusions such as names being shortened, mispronounced, or even laughed at. I finish this section by saying, "These unintentional exclusions are as painful as the more overt forms of discrimination, more so in some ways because they are both ubiquitous and invisible. The bleeding is internal, the emotional labour determining whether to interrupt or to swallow. Either way, there is risk involved."

Still, as the host organization's director comes onstage at the end to thank us presenters, she tries, stutters, and proceeds to grossly mispronounce my name. There are only six of us to thank. For me, getting to this moment is the pinnacle, the accumulation of so many steps up this writing mountain in all types of weather — it's my coming out as an author, and it matters to me that I'm represented as authentically as possible. I have spent the last few years convincing white agents, publishers, and media that actually, no, stories by women of colour have not saturated the market and also, by the way, that what is political by your standards is normal for us. What she's enacting, the fact she has not bothered to get the one word right while I have memorized a speech of over a thousand words to support her event, is not just a one-off. It's a goddamn pattern. I'm conveniently seated in the front row and so I call up to correct her. She does the white woman thing of maintaining control at all costs, pausing awkwardly but unable to stop, apologize, and simply check or correct herself. I hear my own voice fading away in the silence of the auditorium. No one sitting on either side of me risks looking my way. It is contravening deeply entrenched WASP norms to speak out loudly, to interrupt someone (especially onstage), to demand respect. I am the handmaiden here and I have acted out of line. I can feel myself shrink inside, the dull throbbing of my leg echoing throughout my whole body.

Afterward, lost in the sea of white donors, I go over to visit the book table and realize the one request I had made of the organization — to have copies of my book on hand to sell — has been overlooked or forgotten. They do, however, have a book about a white man and his favourite tree, making me momentarily regret that I did not turn out to be a birder or hadn't hiked ten thousand kilometres on the Pacific Crest Trail (white people in nature never fails to sell). A staff person approaches me and abashedly whispers, "The director asked me to come and apologize to you." I look over and see this director nearby, an older woman with blond bobbed hair, drink in hand, talking to an older male donor. As I stare, she throws her head back in flirtatious laughter. "Oh," I respond, wondering what prevents her from closing the two-metre gap between us to apologize to me herself. Suddenly, it's all too much. My eyes fill with tears, and I pivot away, feeling the weight of too many indignities piled on top of my own vulnerability in this space. Back in the hotel room, I carefully unwrap layers of gauze, clean the burn wound, reapply all the bandages (this takes an hour), and lie down to order in food. I'm unsure how I'm going to emotionally survive the rest of this journey, while also being aware of how privileged I am to be here at all.

A few days later I arrive in Vancouver for a prominent writers' festival. After checking into the hotel, I decide to venture into the authors' lounge to see if I can connect with some other writers. Despite being a speaker and educator, I dislike social events if I don't have an assigned role. Like many writers, I like writing about humanity more than experiencing it. There are about twenty people in the room and by the high volume of voices, I assume the mostly older white crowd know each other well. I go over and introduce myself to the festival director, whom I've had contact with over email, but find myself disappointed by her stiff reply. I wonder if it's me, my identity, or the work I do on race and equity issues. She cuts our conversation short and takes me over to introduce me to the only other person of colour in the room. We look at each other awkwardly, both of us implicitly acknowledging the POC ghetto we've just been relegated to. I feel like a separate species and ponder if any white author has ever walked into a room and been introduced to the only other white author there. I go with "never."

After my last event at this festival, two days later, I enter the same lounge for a cup of mint tea. An older white woman comes over to me. "I enjoyed your panel," she says. "You and the other presenter [another Brown woman of a different racial/cultural background] with your brown curly hair looked like you could be cousins. You were both so cute!" I have no words with which to respond. Perhaps, I think, I should lower my head so she can actually pat it. Back in the hotel room, as I change the bandages on my wound, I can see that the skin down to my knee is getting infected. I hunt down and visit a medical centre the next day.

"Take these antibiotics," the white doctor instructs as he hands over the script. "How do I look after the wound?" I ask. "I'm worried about it getting worse." He looks at me for a moment, a burp in the predictable pattern of these visits — his face queries why I am asking for more when he's already given his advice. "Don't worry about it," he snaps. Here, again, is the echo of so many moments picking at the scab on childhood wounds where people in authority — doctors, teachers, camp counsellors, and Girl Guide leaders — were collectively unable or unwilling to hear or address the only question my childhood self was holding on to: *Will this get better?* This question scrabbles about in my chest cavity like the pressure of a small mouse colony, demanding release. I say nothing but silently hear the boomerang of my own words from earlier on this trip: "The bleeding is internal, the emotional labour determining whether to interrupt or to swallow. Either way, there is risk involved."

The antibiotics help, but the wound stays red and inflamed. After a stop in the U.S., I fly back to Edmonton, my adopted city after fleeing Iran. This was the one place I was mentally crossing fingers would not be added to my itinerary. I reluctantly said *yes* when the invitation arrived because it felt destined that in talking about my past I would be invited to confront it. After landing in the airport, I hobble over to the customs line and scramble around in my purse to find passport and ID. I am physically exhausted and feel emotionally raw. It's hard to differentiate between forty-six-year-old and nine-year-old me right now.

I look over to see who the customs official is, a white woman with a head of red hair to her shoulders, fully expecting a third-level inquisition about place of birth and purpose of travelling to the U.S. Instead, she takes a moment to smile at me before looking down. "How do I pronounce your name?" she asks. I feel a small spark ignite in my chest as I tell her. After carefully checking my documents, she hands them back with a bigger smile, shocking me with what comes out of her mouth next: "Welcome home."

This exchange sets off another echo of the past, and I realize that perhaps old wounds of rejection and fear of rejection are being touched so that I can squeeze out any lingering puss of shame. Maybe, if I can, I will be able to more deeply appreciate the ways in which this city and this country were both a landing place and a home. Happiness often coexists with abuse. No human experience is monolithic, and my time after immigrating here also held generosity, support, and good people. I smile back at the attendant and whisper, "Thank you," my eyes filling as I fumble forward.

Speaking in Edmonton is a magnification of all the emotions. The bear jaws in my leg sink deeper while the mice in my chest scurry faster. I want to press the eject button from my own body. My first event is in a large downtown mall. I assume the interview is going to be broadcast from the local radio station, but instead I find out there is no recording, and this will instead be a live conversation to be held in the two chairs set up at the entrance of the studio facing the open mall. I meet my interviewer, a young white woman who is clearly new in her role, and wonder if she has even opened my book. A few minutes later, as we are seated in front of our tiny audience with mall shoppers moving to and fro behind them, she lobs the opening question toward me. "You write about the trauma of moving here to Canada" — there is a burst of background noise as a group of people enter the mall doors — "CAN YOU TELL US WHAT IT WAS LIKE FOR YOU AS A CHILD BEING SPAT ON AND GOING TO THE BATHROOM MULTIPLE TIMES EACH NIGHT?"

I pause to let the background cacophony die down so I can hear my own voice responding. This question, in this environment, is like being thrown into the freezing ocean in the middle of a storm. As I bypass shock in an effort to get my bearings and start swimming in some direction toward shore, I try to internally decipher what layers of the past I wish to reveal. Do I launch into years of being told I smelled, of being called racial slurs, or of being shunned so severely that even momentary eye contact could make my whole day? How do I unravel years of social rejection, chapters in the book, into words that my body and this random group of strangers can hold? I realize that this flailing around, trying to grab onto the right words as a lifesaver to reach shores of safety and understanding, is how I've always felt in this place. I wonder what kind of cosmic joke is being played on me.

That evening, as part of another festival event, I'm onstage between an older white female author and a new Indigenous writer. The white woman answers in spurts of minutes while I and the other author try and squeeze between and around her long-winded responses. Like in most election debates, the moderators lack basic moderator skills. I have learned to be the participant-moderator at many of these events. At the signing table immediately afterward, there is a lineup of people to buy books. I'm grateful — that's the point of all this. The first person comes up and says, "It sounds like you had a hard childhood, but you must be glad it happened, because you're here." Another one comments, "Canada is a great place to move to, don't you think?" And yet another, "You're so pretty! I hope you know how beautiful you are." I realize that I have to make peace with white people's discomfort with the content of my book. Either I'm the hero or victim, pain-free or in need of rescuing, all designed to make the witness feel better. This is the legacy of discrimination — you never get to choose who you are, and the choices are usually a dehumanizing dichotomy with no room in-between for the nuances of personhood. These people aren't aware that they hold positions of identity privilege. They dictate the culture, and whiteness as a culture is suffocating.

I go to the bathroom and check my email. My editor has sent a message letting me know he's recommended me to do a book review for a national publication. We are an unlikely union, he and I — the white, urban hipster and the older, racialized activist — but I also know I wouldn't be here without his belief in me. Amid the struggle is also reuniting with an old but dear friend from university, and we have the conversation we were unable to have back then: what it was like in our minority racial identities to grow up here. Our evening ends with us giggling in the back seat of my father's small Honda SUV as he stops at a green light, accelerating on my prompt to move forward at a speedy twenty kilometres an hour. My dad is a terrible driver. Some things do not change. We don't stop laughing until we arrive at her house. Every moment feels full of so much emotion, with so much richness to digest.

I try to focus on feeling grateful for these moments of connection and support, but the overwhelming combination of being in so much of my past with this present that doesn't feel so very different takes a toll. The next morning, I visit yet another medical centre. The doctor enters the room like a religious figure about to perform last rites and vigorously pulls away the bandages protecting the injured area. I look at my leg spread out like a skinned animal carcass awaiting dissection. He turns away in shock or disgust (I can't tell) and barks, "You need to come in every day to get this taken care of!" I feel like he is blaming me for the burn. The nurse proceeds to scrub all the remaining bits of dead skin from the wound as I suck in my breath. "Debridement," the nurse says, apropos of nothing. In response to my questioning look, she expands, "It means cleaning the wound of all foreign objects." I wonder if I am the foreign object here or what foreign objects I still need to exorcise from within.

A week later, after returning home to Toronto in-between travels, I get a last-minute call to attend a prestigious literary event at the Four Seasons Hotel in the upscale Yorkville neighbourhood. I feel again the expectation of being honoured (and again, I am), but I'm also running on fumes at this point after back-to-back events educating mostly white audiences about the reality of racism. There is one author to be placed at each event sponsor's table with twelve other people who each pay over a thousand dollars to attend. I get an image of petting animals at the zoo. I tell the event's organizer that I'm hesitant about spending the night surrounded by rich white people who have no connection to my book. I don't know if I have it in me to parlay concepts like race, immigration, and exile into light dinner conversation. I hear his voice in my ear assuring me that I will be well taken care of and that, in fact, I will be at the same table as the association president. The president is, they continue confidently, delighted to have me there and looking forward to personally welcoming me.

I make an appointment to have my hair done and find myself later that evening in a fancy cream-and-gold ballroom seated between a white woman, who is head of HR for a large company, and a young gay white man who turns out to be extremely funny. I'm grateful for them both, realizing that this is some kind of awkward for most of us, and we all have our ways of overcompensating. The meal passes while prizes are handed out onstage by white people to mostly other white people, although there are banners of diverse authors hovering behind the stage like ghosts. Margaret Atwood is mentioned so often it's clear that here in the country of Canadian literature she is the queen, and I wonder what happens to those of us who genuflect incorrectly. The event is almost over when the association president's name is announced by the person onstage. I think, *She must be sick this evening,* but no, this elegant woman with long blond hair *across the table from me* stands and waves her arm to the crowded room of about three hundred plus people. I can't help but stare at her as she sits back down, but she doesn't return my gaze. Why would she start now?

The magnitude of her oversight bangs through the defences I have built up, and suddenly I again feel my irrelevance. She, who heads this prestigious writers' organization, whose support I was explicitly promised, has not even bothered to lean over to introduce herself, to introduce me, or to offer any other kind of welcome even though I am the sole author and only person of colour seated at this table. This moment becomes a metaphor for the house of Canadian writers I have come to visit for the first time with this first book. I, and the other racialized writers I can see scattered at tables around the room, are present but unseen. We are wooed for the colour we represent, but we don't yet belong.

I overhear an announcement from the stage announcing the next association president newly coming into the position, and to my surprise it is an older white man who comes to the microphone. *Is this really happening?* Every single literary association, almost every writers' festival, and most publishing houses in this country are still led by white people born and raised in Canada, and despite the best of efforts, if you're here you'd better know how to use the salad fork. There is no hand eating, floor seating, or kids running amok in spaces like these. White culture is the perfectionism of skin and bone hidden behind polite masks and polished with emotionally neutral conversation. I have to strait-jacket so much of myself to be here, and I am tired of playing the role of grateful author.

As the evening formalities wind down and the others at my table start drifting off (the president still has not made eye contact), I remain seated amid the white tablecloths and elaborate flower bouquets. I think about how writing my story in the form of a book and putting it out into the world is like removing layers of skin. No surprise that I burned myself.

Was it worth it? I wonder. *Is* it worth it?

I think about the way racism — and scalding water — have permanently marked me, but finding these words — *telling the story* — has resurrected me and guided me forward. If immigrating to Canada was the original burn, shame became the foreign object. My book is my form of debridement, my battle cry for a future where everyone has access to belonging, where authors of every identity and background will share their stories with an equally diverse readership. I am part of this colour-full revolution, and as I think this I look up to see two well-known women of colour authors dancing up on the stage, their shadows looming large on the wall behind them. They wave at me and I wave back. I remember that belonging is usually fought for, in some countries with weapons, in this country with our words. A sense of home is often messy and it can be complicated, but home is also where we choose to settle down for the struggle and lick our wounds before showing up to start anew the next day, to continue the story or to write a new beginning.

In the cab at the end of the night, I think back to my last medical visit in Toronto a few days earlier. As I lay on the white operating surface, the doctor peered over my leg with the care of a midwife mid-delivery, gingerly prodding the delicate skin. I hear her voice echo in my ear softly. "It's certainly healing." I let out a breath I didn't know I'd been holding, to hear her add, "slowly."

COURAGE

My book is coming out in two weeks. On the inside I feel like one of those overeager washing machines that spins so wildly it shakes the house and I'd swear it's about to launch into outer space.

I didn't expect myself to have this reaction. You publish a memoir because you HAVE SOMETHING TO SAY. You write while your kid naps and you write much later at night than the next day is going to forgive you for. You write drafts in your head while shopping for groceries and voice record them in the car on the way home. Yelling to your partner — "Just a sec! I need a minute!" — you scramble madly to finish typing as you hide out in the bathroom, late for dinner once again. In other words, it's a commitment. The process of writing, editing, and polishing your story changes you. It makes you rest into the words you've written and think, *Yes, that's true*, and slowly you realize you've mostly written what your own soul needs to graduate from the university of the past. It's a gift; it is humbling.

And then, just when you think you've arrived at the planet called rest or success or achievement, you realize the writing was only the beginning, because now you have to speak to people about this journey that wrung you from the inside out, translating it into pretty words that people can relate to. I keep hearing, "You must be so excited, your book is coming out soon!" And I am. But also … I am terrified. I feel so fucking raw. I thought writing a book was insurance against ever feeling this vulnerable again. What if it's not good enough? What if I offend people or, worse, get attacked? What if I get locked back into emotional solitary confinement? My rational mind is on hiatus while that tender underbelly reminds me to go slow, to set the machine to the longest cycle so the different parts of me have time to get clean of the fear.

I am ready. I am not ready. I am ready. I am not ready. How do you prepare for something you know will change your life but you've never experienced before? You don't. You just hang on, knowing the cycle will end at some point, and trust that you'll be the better for having the courage to hold on for dear life.

And then, maybe, if you're lucky, you'll have your launch at the largest art gallery in your country, in the middle of your city, in the room with the largest windows, and you'll sit illuminated onstage, and you'll find your speaking voice, and then, after, you'll see a younger woman stand up (could be you from the past with her brown curly mane) and stammer out, "I didn't have words for what I went through until I read this, thank you" — THANK YOU — and you collect all the kind words that come your way from that point onwards and load them up into that mental washing machine, filling it up, getting ready to set it for another spin.

Because what you remember now is that the spin keeps you alive, the around and around loosening the fear so you're not held hostage so tightly, some of those demons released from emotional purgatory at last. You realize that although the book is about you, it's *not* you, because you are the story, and the story is as big as the galaxy, as unknowable as these stars, and always, always turning.

TRICKSTER

Over breakfast I catch Arion stealing her brother's share of the cranberries, the garnish for our breakfast oatmeal. I bend down and tease her. "You little trickster! Just like Anansi!" And I launch into an animated description of Anansi, the trickster spider character originating in Ghana that spread to other Caribbean cultures. This conversation spreads to Carnival and soca dancing, which harken from the same cultural roots. I pull up some videos of Carnival, and we watch enraptured at the sight of all these bodies, different colours and sizes, writhing en masse like a moving rainbow through the streets. My daughter starts to dance in tandem or, at least, as close as she is able to imitate. But I have to use caution because although I want her to have a literacy of diverse cultures, of ways of being in the world that are not centred in whiteness, these are not our cultural roots. I don't want to exoticize the unfamiliar, to pull out another's cultural traditions as entertainment disguised under the banner of diversity. It's a fine line.

And so, as we're getting ready for school a few minutes later, I follow up with, "Have you ever talked about Anansi or Carnival at school?"

"No," they both respond, unsurprisingly.

"Why do you think that is," I ask, "when we know so much about Christmas and Easter and ballroom dancing?"

They look at me with blank faces. No conversation about other cultures can happen without noticing the presence of power as well:

Has this culture historically had the access to tell its own truths?

Do we see members of this culture on our screens, in our papers, in our friendship circles?

Have we ever listened to someone from this culture tell us their story, and more importantly has it changed us?

White people's stories have been repeated over and over again until they become "normal," but others, like Anansi, have to trick their way into popular culture, reminding us to shake up our proprietorial hold on reality.

We cannot steal moves without honouring their origins. We cannot divorce a people from their culture, stories, dances, and celebrations as we pick what parts to consume and which to bury. In the stories we tell and how we tell them, we choose our role of colonizer or liberator.

RESCUE

I'm on the plane in Vancouver, ready to fly home after a three-week book tour of so many people and readings and questions I'm squeezed fresh out of juice. My head is pounding with an early migraine, and I'm starting to feel nauseous. An older, white-haired couple carefully make their way into the two seats beside me, apologizing for the inconvenience as they fold themselves in. I exhale, relieved at their surface friendliness.

I tell them that I was in town for a writers' festival. They are on their way to a conference where he is speaking about investment capital. I am not of interest enough for him to make further conversation, so he folds into his newspaper while she dives in to ask me what my book is about. I reply, "It's about my journey immigrating here, facing racism, and the lifelong journey to recover myself." I'm hoping I can get away with just this one-liner.

She hesitates, then asks, "Were your experiences of immigration positive?"

I wonder how she got this from what I said as I fake laugh (charmingly, I think) and respond, "Not quite, one usually doesn't write memoir from a place of happiness."

She offers a carefree chuckle as well. And then, "Where did you immigrate from?"

"Iran," I answer. And then we enter the landscape that is so familiar and yet demoralizing because now I am no longer simply another stranger on the plane but someone who represents an entire ethnic group. The pressure is on.

"Ooooh, that country has gone through a lot."

"It's the one place I've always wanted to travel to."

"Dashtgard isn't a Persian name, is it?"

"Have you gone back?"

"Do you speak the language?"

"My husband invests in a lot of Persian-run businesses."

"They are so hard-working. Wonderful people. So generous."

It's not that her questions are not well intended, it's that I feel I've gone from a person to an object, defined by my edges rather than the substance underneath. I know she wants my story, but I can't tell it right now.

Just because I wrote a book doesn't mean the story is always accessible, especially when I have to translate so it doesn't threaten white people's sense of our country as a multicultural oasis and myself as a grateful immigrant. I could say I'm not feeling well (true) but like many women, especially women of colour who too often require white people's approval to get by, it's ingrained in me to look after another's feelings over my own. There are four more hours of plane ride to go.

I pick up a pen, knowing I can safely disappear into imagination where I can be anyone and all parts of myself simultaneously, a reminder that although I can't control what happens to me and around me, I have power over how it will shape me, the story I will tell.

KINTSUGI

To write is to spend time reading, not merely books (that's the easy part), but the world.

It requires slowing down enough to notice the way your mother's eyes wrinkle at the corners when she drinks her cup of tea, and the way these lines deepen year by year until they slowly appear in the same place on your own face.

It's feeling the hard pressure of your daughter's arms squeezing into your middle-age belly to say goodbye for the third time before parting ways, knowing soon she will forgo even a wave before she heads out the door.

It's watching leaves bud, and dance, and fall, year after year, some years the leaves becoming lives.

To read the world, to really read it, is to be broken over and over again.

But it is also to remember that brokenness is not the end of this story, and a writer's job is the practice of the Japanese art of kintsugi — filling the cracks with words that shine like gold, turning scars into shimmering rivers we can all trace back to the sea.

8

RACIAL IMPOSTER

This year, summer has been a dog chasing its own tail, one hot day outshining the next until melting or evaporating seem the only possible outcomes. It's the end of the season, and we've booked one last hurrah at the amusement park on Centre Island, a local attraction and kid heaven with enough vintage charm and natural beauty to satisfy adult tastes as well. Today is a perfect end-of-summer day, the slight wind and frothy waters a gentle backdrop to the child-led cacophony surrounding us as we sail over on the ferry. I'm going with my close friend, a white woman with a nine-year-old daughter the same age as mine. My seven-year-old son, Koda, and his friend are along, too.

Once we arrive I instruct the children: "If you get separated from us, go and find someone who works at one of the rides or the eating places. Ask them for help." My son is turned away, wrestling with his friend, so I tug his arm to bring his eyes to my mine. "Did you hear me?" I ask. He nods quickly before racing off.

After lining up for three rides over a two-hour window, I'm starting to fade and notice it's lunchtime, the parent in me well aware food is needed to stave off potential emotional meltdowns. My friend and I wait in another long lineup to load up with hot dogs and pizza slices. We find an abandoned group of picnic tables alongside one of the buildings and dump our cardboard food packages across the roughened wood surface. My stomach grumbles as I sit down.

Then it begins. My son starts whining that his sister got more of the lemonade than he did. I wonder what I was thinking buying a sugary drink (and then remember it was meant for me). She responds by grabbing a couple of his fries. In his anger, he wallops her on the arm and she hits him back (no time wasted). Meanwhile, I am curling up inside with embarrassment, all cells gearing up to move forward and somehow confine this loud and seemingly non-normative behaviour. Both the other children are sitting watching mine with enormous, rounded eyes. I am aware of my friend seated beside me, averting her gaze. As command snaps into my voice, I imagine the watching children's eyes getting even bigger. In the Brown culture that I grew up in (and that still exists in most parts of the world today), children were swatted for bad behaviour like this. Without corporeal punishment to rely on, there's not much left in the tool kit!

My son stomps off to another table, and I let him go, my nervous system already on edge because of their arguing. I gulp back a couple of bites before he returns, his face scrunched in a frown as he immediately grabs his sister's glass to take a drink, setting off the argument again, which now turns into a chase around the table. Getting up to intervene, I haul my son away by the arm, knowing the only hope for peace is to separate and soothe.

If I were at a family get-together or, really, any one of a number of Brown people events, this would be normal behaviour. Here, in polite white Canadian society, it is not, and while trying to stuff my children back into their cultural straitjackets, I realize I've gone into fight-or-flight mode. The embarrassment has escalated to shame. I'm pushing to make them fit in as I tried so desperately to do, pulled between white and Brown cultural norms, torn between British and Persian parents.

It takes me until after another two rides, when we're standing in the longest lineup so far and my chicks are still chirping the loudest, to bow out and take refuge on a nearby bench. Between their antics and the intense heat, I'm getting dizzy.

I sit back, breathe, and watch the cornflower blue of the passing sky, feel the faint breeze whispering past. Slowly moving back into sync with myself, I start mentally rewinding the day. It hits me in a moment of sudden clarity, a bird's wing cutting through hazy thought clouds, that this is a familiar state. I recognize this bone-level exhaustion. This is the "tired of being me" identity fatigue that happens for many mixed-race or biracial folks that are a mix of white/non-white or oppressor/marginalized. When faced with the choice of what racial identity — British/white or Persian/Brown — to inhabit, if there's a mismatch between my cultural expression and the setting I'm in, I lift out and away as my body continues on automatic pilot mode. We still live in a society that needs people to fit into neatly established categories. To be caught between two cultures that are not equal in expression or acceptance creates a very real and constant internal friction. Which identity to inhabit isn't just a choice, it's a trauma, each one with different consequences either internally or externally. I finally name what I've been circling for years; this state is *identity dissociation*.

❋

Moving from Iran, from familiar cultural waters, to white-led North America was the start of experiencing passive policing from those around me. At that time white stopped being acknowledged as a race, but Brown somehow *was*. However, this isn't just about those with white/European skin colour having an advantage, but about WASP culture being considered normal, the cultural default setting. My olive skin with Middle Eastern features marked me as different in the all-white neighbourhood I grew up in, but it was as much my personality, with its neon Persian colours screaming she's too loud/confident/bossy, that was the marker of difference. It's often hard to know where reactions toward race end and culture begin.

Culture is the most powerful influence on our sense of belonging; it's what we all accept as "normal" or as the implicitly superior way of being and interacting. The cultural norms in Canadian society are diametrically opposed to the Middle Eastern culture I was brought up in. The one-size-fits-all version of four nuclear family members never quite fit our sometimes never-ending extended family structure (try buying a family pass anywhere). There is a gap between the high value placed on quiet and avoidance of conflict versus assertively sharing one's opinion — it's the loudest, not the most informed, who's right in my family. Finally, WASP culture is all about boundaries and the careful accounting of property and money versus the overwhelming generosity and *ta'aroofing* that marks Persian society. Canadian society is still orchestrated like a classical piano piece whereas I was used to rock music. The take-away: turn yourself down.

I absorbed the unspoken belief that the more you culturally assimilate, the less your racial difference will matter. This culture of a certain form of commodified whiteness is hard for many folks of various ethnicities whose heritages are subsumed under a generic white banner. But it's harder for those who are white-adjacent. Many mixed-race people try and fit in, buying into the illusion that by acting WASPy they will be treated as white, with some succeeding more than others. But our differences always catch us in the end.

As I sit on the bench I recall a recent visit to a local music store to pick up a violin for my daughter's upcoming school year. As soon as we walked in, my daughter gravitated (not surprisingly) to the drum set section and started banging away with surprising ability. The drums were rubber so the sound was mostly muted. I gave her five minutes before wresting her away to focus on the task at hand. She was her usual loud and brash self as she examined the violin while getting distracted by the keyboard nearby, and once we were finished, she made a mad dash back to the drums. During our time together, the white male sales clerk's expression moved from forced politeness to strained.

As he returned with the violin, my daughter reached a crescendo with the drums. I'd tried to move her off a couple of times, to no avail. In her I have met my match. She is as strong-willed as I am, and that was not the place for a power struggle. I figured I would let her enjoy the novelty — there were only a couple others in the store and the sound wasn't offensive. Yet as I looked back, I caught a full-fledged frown on the face of the man helping us and immediately translated this into "God, these people! What mother lets her daughter be so loud and rambunctious. A 'good' or 'proper' or 'white' parent would have their child under control." Here, again, like multiple moments in every day, I was reminded that white culture is synonymous with control, perfectionism, and quiet, which in many ways is the polar opposite of my temperament formed in the cauldron of Persian culture. While paying for her instrument, I was internally stressed between trying to appease the sales clerk and feeling angry at his entitlement to act so surly with me. This stress is part of the emotional background of my life.

My thoughts immediately jump to another time where I was invited to speak on a renowned TV panel. I wore a body-hugging red dress with black polka dots and 4-inch, black patent heels. I looked professional-hot, even by my own high standards. One of my staff, James, who is a close-to-six-foot white guy around my age, met me there. His jeans were covered with mud splatters, and he had a backpack slung over his shoulder as he'd biked over during a surprise rain shower. We were ushered into the green room before going in to tape the show. One young male staff person came in and walked right over to James to shake his hand and say "Welcome." I got a nod. The second person came in, similar looking to the first, and once again went to shake James's hand. This time I got a smile to accompany the nod. Finally, a third woman came in and also went to shake James's hand. By this point, he and I were both feeling uncomfortable, and he pointed to me and said, "It's actually Annahid who's here for the interview." The woman made her way over to give me the benefit of the long-awaited handshake greeting.

Inside I was seething and felt my confidence starting to sag. I wondered if they had a call sheet and if my name had been confused for a man. Or if the more insidious truth held, that despite my clothes signalling high status, they still didn't overcome the liability of my gender and race in that room. No matter how much I know, or what I wear, or my name being on a call sheet, I have never been greeted first when I'm next to a white person, and if my companion is also male, it takes even more effort to get recognized. Later that night, I texted an acquaintance who worked there to share what happened. She, a white woman, responded with great surprise, saying she'd heard complaints of women facing occasional gender harassment but no complaints about race. I wondered how many people of colour worked there. I wondered how many spoke up. I went to bed that night feeling deeply alone.

And then I remember the dream. One of those where you wake up feeling like your soul is sending a memo to your brain. I had received a diagnosis that I was going to die, and very soon. After the chance to say goodbye to my people, I entered the hospital. But instead of dying, I gave life to a blond, chubby baby boy. The baby wasn't needy at all. He was calm, cherubic, and easy to love. A friend's white husband came to visit. He remained nameless and faceless. He followed me into the bathroom, and as I was undressing I found him peeping at my vagina under the bathroom stall door. I screamed "Go away!" and instead he started to push the door in. Meanwhile the little blond baby was waddling around, charming all the people in the hallway nearby. The dream seemed to communicate that the darker "different" me was dying to allow the white part of myself to stay alive by innocently toddling around and making people smile.

No matter how hard I try to master WASP behaviour and charm my way through this white society, the other part continues to live in fear of invisible assault. Because it *is* an assault — to the very shape of self. Whether I'm appearing on TV, taking my children on an outing, going for a walk through my neighbourhood, I regularly encounter moments of being underestimated, my intelligence and knowledge downgraded or dismissed, my behaviour judged more harshly. Then if I speak out about the ways I experience these subtle layers of racism in the white dominant spaces I exist in, I'm ignored or attacked. I've been berated while dropping off my children to school, met with silence repeatedly when bringing up the topic of race, ignored when walking down the street. We can talk about gender but we still cannot talk about race.

Over time, I got used to being an island, at sea in the different communities I found myself in.

Now I know that being mixed race comes with the highest rates of race-related depression and anxiety because of that absence of a singular community to identify with. It's the constant tightrope walking, the ever-present anxiety of "Am I too much or not enough?" that leads to a gradual haunting by the ghosted parts of ourselves. Like many biracial and mixed-race people I learned to code-switch, to be adaptable with what parts of myself to showcase in which environments, usually grinding down to extinction the foreign part of myself in the mostly white academic and, later, professional environments I found myself in. But when the more colourful Persian part comes in through a strong opinion, raised voices, or my kids' unruly behaviour, and I can't bottle it or control it, that's when I start abandoning myself. We can't stay dissociated from, or eternally suppress, essential parts of who we are. Our differences always catch us in the end.

❋

I look up to see my friend walking over to tell me the kids have run over from the roller coaster to the petting zoo. Getting up, I teeter slightly off balance. I realize I'm still feeling emotionally fragmented and plan ahead for our departure. I walk over to go and round up the kids. The nearby animal enclosure is small, making it easy to track down my volume-perpetually-on-high-voiced daughter with her quieter friend. My son's friend, too, is nearby, bent over, petting a goat. I ask him where Koda is and he looks up blank-faced. "I don't know. I thought he was beside me." We all search idly for a few minutes and then more urgently. I'm not yet panicked, but I am moving in that direction. I direct everyone to fan out in a different direction. I'm also feeling the slow creep of shame that twice in one day I've lost control over my willful kids.

After five minutes of searching against a backdrop of screeching children and picnicking tourists, we come back together: still no Koda. By now my heart is pumping wildly as I churn over the options. My daughter starts to sob: "What if we never find him, Mama?" Her friend puts an arm around her. My son's friend, too, is worried, running back and forth bleating, "Koda, Koda!" As I lift my eyes trying to feel inwardly for guidance on the next step, it occurs to me to check my phone. Indeed there's a strange number that I immediately press to call back. "We've found your son," the unidentifiably accented voice says into my ear. "He came to the hotdog stand and announced to us that he was lost." My body sags in relief that he remembered my instructions. And with flair, too. My kids' lack of boundaries is actually a superpower.

As I see my son walking toward us, I grin maniacally and wave my arm back and forth, not caring how Persian I appear in this moment. What if ... What if my kids and I are really the "normal" ones? What if it's healthier to have a sense of belonging that is not pinned down to one context, one way of behaving or one cultural set of rules? What *would* it be like if others could stretch invisible inclusion muscles by asking themselves:

Is this behaviour making me uncomfortable because it's wrong or because it's just not what I'm used to?

Could this behaviour that is different serve to enrich this classroom, conversation, boardroom?

How can I lean into unfamiliar cultural interactions to prevent another moment of micro-oppression where this person is forced to give up who they are — to racially dissociate — to be in relationship with me?

Everyone loses when one way of being is made out as superior to all other ways, where one group of people is believed to be superior to other groups. Most of us know this consciously — it's catching the subconscious patterns where the work lies. What if instead of *identity dissociation* we cultivate *identity wholeness*, allowing people to express differences without those differences appearing as a threat.

※

As Koda runs straight over to hug me and I wrap him in tight against me, I wonder when I'll get to the point that I'll be able to welcome all parts of myself with open arms and when, even further in the distant future, that will be possible in society. Belonging in a mixed identity is not only about constantly negotiating what part of oneself to occupy internally, but also what parts to accept and advocate for while in community. I can allow the white part of me to wander freely around soaking up people's favour because she is infant-like: deferential and non-threatening. But more importantly in the belonging stakes is learning to take the side of the traumatized Persian part of myself, in a corner inside recovering from years of emotional violence, and let her out of the box. I'm getting better at it, and at relinquishing the consequences.

Fifty years from now, mixed identity people will form the majority in North America, as well as increasing exponentially across the globe. What will be lost if these future beings continue marginalizing their racial and cultural differences to act more white than the people around them, just as many women entering the workforce think they can succeed only if they act more "male" than the men around them? Inclusion isn't sacrificing our differences to succeed, it is having access to success *because* of those differences.

My biracial identity has not weakened me. It's my gift in my work and in the world: I make the invisible nature of power, visible. I help people see what has been lost in our monoculture and what we will gain by welcoming contrast. What would our world be if we eliminated the exuberant green and blues from the visual palette surrounding us? Creating cultures of belonging where we all access all parts of our multiple intelligences, brilliance, compassion, and creativity is my vision of utopia, and I dream into it, lean into it, fight like hell for it, every day. Our differences can save us in the end.

※

It's getting late in the afternoon as I take Koda's hand and pull him over to the bench to sit beside me. The sun beams down upon our dark heads bent in toward each other, but we don't notice, caught in our own loving glow. Beyond identity, all people today have shown up with innate goodness: my friend who has patiently allowed me to take a break, these children's concern for their absent friend, the hotdog seller who walked my son back over but also, people staffing these rides, park keepers, and fellow parents who together bestow magic on this island. I feel a rush of warmth (for once not due to this heat) for the gift of being alive here, now, in this place. Eventually we make our way over to the lineup of folks waiting for the ferry ready to transport us off this island and return us home. I hope that identity in the future is this easy: a shuttling back and forth, no holds barred, all of us able to travel across cultural borders to learn what we don't yet know, to be enriched by differences foreign yet exquisite, and to be reminded that connection once lost, can be restored.

GAPS

"My twelve-year-old son asked me if there would be any Brown or Black kids in his class this year," says the black-haired, pale-faced woman seated at the table in front of me. She goes on to add, "I said, 'Yes,' which settled him down. Honestly, I didn't think about his skin colour being different until this last year of Black Lives Matter protests. I never thought he was aware of it. I don't know why he's making it such a big deal."

As she talks about her bi-racial son, I'm standing a mere metre away, yet at an emotional distance of generations. Experiencing my own flashbacks, I wonder why it is so hard for white mothers to acknowledge racial difference — darker skin — as a primary factor shaping their child's journey through the world.

Do they fear not being able to protect their child?

Do they fear eventual distance between them and their child because of racial differences?

Do they perhaps feel that racial discrimination is not as significant as gender inequality?

I wonder why racial differences are so hard for parents to acknowledge? If a child has a disability, many parents rush to understand and set up supports so their child will not be isolated in their experience.

I am mentally scrambling for what to say. Do I educate her from a place of professional expertise as CEO of a racial justice organization? Or do I share my own experience growing up as a biracial child encountering racism, with a white mother who found it hard to relate, resulting in a lifetime spent overcoming the belief that I was the problem? Do I simply empathize, and throw the conversational ball forward to another moment in the future?

Yet this woman could be my mother. She is so many mothers. She is the fastest growing demographic of mothers who do not share their children's racial or mixed heritage. She represents a vast parenting group who are so well intentioned and yet simply don't get it. I don't want to reduce this moment to a pedagogical lesson. Nor do I want to pretend nothing is at stake.

I am at stake here, too.

I finally respond, "It's a good thing he's asking these questions. His journey through the world will be different from yours, and the more you know about what he's going through being Black, the easier it will be for him."

Loving someone does not mean an equalizing of experience. Love merely offers a kind of courage to push open the door between worlds, so we are more likely to learn what lies on the other side for our beloved. Fierce love means stretching into the places of difference rather than defaulting to the oppressive expectation of sameness.

LANGUAGE

I am about to tentatively read aloud my almost indecipherable Arabic handwriting. I'm halfway through this third Farsi language class in downtown Toronto with a handful of other students. To my left is the blond weightlifter who wants to learn some words to impress her Iranian boyfriend's parents (read: mother), and to my right is a well-dressed gal about a decade younger, who appears to have had the ubiquitous Persian nose job. I start reading: "*Kheli mamnoon. Man mikhouram …*" (Thank you very much. I'm eating …). Once I'm finished, our recently immigrated Persian teacher repeats everything I've just read, correcting my accent. Nose Girl's lips twitch as she looks down.

Then it's her turn. She reads her paragraph flawlessly. I inwardly roll my eyes, irritated that though she was born in Canada she's had more access to the language, and it shows. When I was growing up, many first-generation immigrant parents often held back speaking in the mother tongue, afraid it would hinder getting ahead in English. Though born in Iran, I can't out accent her. "*Kheili khub!*" (Very good!), our teacher exclaims after Nose Girl's finished.

I inwardly sigh in defeat. I know I'll never win in the stakes of who's more Persian here. No, I correct myself. I am ahead of Wrestler Woman. We have to take small victories where we can.

Later, as the teacher comes around to inspect our handwriting, Nose Girl once again gets a "*Kheli khub!*" (the verbal gold star), and I see her smile as she nods in acknowledgement. As the teacher walks by my desk she stops and looks down. I wait for her recognition of my painstakingly zealous curls and dots dancing from right to left across the page. "Ooh, what a wonderful colour that is. Where did you find that pen?"

I dare not look at Nose Girl this time.

As I'm the last to pack up at the end of class — at least proficient in the Persian art of tardiness — I hear Nose Girl call her goodbye, "*Khodah hafez*," a perfect deep throat *kh* sound that is the mark of a true Persian speaker (just as *th* marks native English speakers). I smile wanly and respond in kind, internally wincing once again at my pronunciation.

It's only later (I'd like to say days or weeks but, really, it was years) that I can fully own how jealous I was (perhaps still am) of Nose Girl and others like her who were born here and lost less, who can take who they are for granted. Language connects them to a culture and place I mostly feel the absence of. No matter how hard I try, I know I will never come across as fully and "authentically" Persian.

Here's my secret: it's true that I don't have a lot of time these days to relearn Farsi, but the deeper truth is that I don't have the emotional energy required to work through all the feelings attached to the language — loss, frustration, irritation, and failure. Language can be a bridge, but starting on fresh ground is different from rebuilding a broken structure covering a graveyard of losses. Farsi, for me, is a haunted language, and I'm too busy breaking barriers in every other part of life to stay here busting ghosts. I foster a connection to Persian culture through words and food, family and celebration. I have accepted my own definition of what it means to be culturally Persian, and language is only a part of it.

I do still use that purple colour though, and sometimes I can be found whispering, "*Kheli khub*," to myself after a piece of good writing — even when it's not in the language of my homeland.

PEARLS

Canada is an adopted parent. Iran, my motherland, would not recognize the self I have grown into nor would the other ancestor, England, for different reasons. Like any adoptee, I search the world for a place to call my own but have found there is no single or easy answer, only an increasingly complicated set of desires to see myself reflected, to use cultural shorthands with those around me.

I have not found homogeneity but perhaps I have found something more valuable: a flexibility of identity, a fluidity of what home can mean, an in-between place that keeps me close to the edge of emptiness, so that I never take connection for granted.

I've learned to grab and hold on to the moments of acceptance and connection within my adopted family, turning them over in memory, polishing them to perfection, until they sit as glistening pearls around my neck, reminders of the circular path to belonging, that wholeness sneaks up on us step by rounded step.

9

BOSS LADY

'm the boss now, unkempt curls and all. We've recently upgraded from a polo quartet to a rugby team, and it sure feels rougher out here. Given that we *teach* leadership skills, I thought moving into a weightier management role would be a slam dunk, but it's different when you're the captain on the court, hustling in the championship playoffs. I'm reminded daily that knowing something is not the same as being able to practise it. Being in a leadership role is different from being a leader. I know exercise is important, I don't do it often enough. I know listening, supporting, and trusting others are important leadership elements, and I'm not doing these enough either. My new CEO coach tells me about a client of his who, when asked the secret to his success, responded, "Learning to shut up." This has become my new mantra.

I ask our Chief Operating Officer (COO) for feedback after every staff meeting so that I can learn and improve. Today's dose:

"Your framing in the beginning of the meeting was really great. You gave the right amount of information and it was inspiring." Score one for me, I think, but then she continues. "Yet later, you interrupted me when I was talking about the new hires, and I felt undermined. You did the same when you suggested who should be assigned to x project. I'm managing the team now; you should check with me first."

"Okaaay," I respond almost automatically, adding a belated, "thank you." Inside, though, I'm thinking, *Ugh, fuck! Why can't I just have the freedom to be myself? How much more of this do I have to take?!* And inevitably, *Would this feedback be the same if I were a white man?* As someone who is still fighting for visibility and credibility as a first-generation immigrant woman of colour in a world where I interact mostly with white middle-aged men and women, I'm used to facing a gap in power because of my racial and gender identity. I feel the weight of constant auditioning for the expert role, and though I usually nail the performance, I wish it were assumed more easily.

I don't say any of this to our COO, though. I know that as the boss I need to hold a different relationship to power, because rather than having to fight for it here, it's a given. Though I notice when bias might be colouring someone's words or actions toward me, it's a lot harder to see where I unintentionally harm others because of my own biases. It's a psychological truth that we protect parts of ourselves where we've been hurt, so it's a whole lot easier to see where we *don't* have power than where we do. As humans we're constantly jostling to get noticed, trying to get into the club, to unquestionably *belong*. We're often unaware how we push others out of the way to get there. Learning to use our power well means seeing it not as currency, but as part of the very air we breathe. Where is it hard for us to take a deep breath, but as importantly, where do we breathe more easily than those around us? The balance of power can shift

sometimes moment to moment. In this new role I'm committed
to a massive power upgrade, hoping it doesn't completely blow my
ego fuse.

It took me a long time to get to the point where I'm able to ask for
and receive this kind of feedback, to be confronted with a different
story from the one I tell myself. When I was twenty-five, I travelled across the country to our nation's capital for one of my first
grown-up jobs: organizing a national campaign for a large social
justice organization. It was a dream come true. At the time, I was
one of the only non-white staff in a group of about thirty. I didn't
think it would be a big deal to move far away from family and community, but it was. My body, as it always did, took the hit for the
double blows of separation and increased isolation. I didn't know
how to touch my feelings, never mind express them, so they came
out through self-harm behaviour. My body was a site I could always
control, in contrast to the lack of control I felt externally. The bulimia — daily bingeing and purging — only increased the longer I
was in the job. I'd excel at work and let out all the supressed feelings
over a toilet bowl at the end of the day.

Toward the end of my first year, the organization I was working
for introduced a new performance management system — a 360
review, which meant that rather than just getting feedback from a
single manager, everyone around was asked to pipe in as well. Up
until that point I felt like the new wunderkind, everyone amazed by
what I'd been able to pull off: a panel of high-profile speakers, cross-
country events, and coast-to-coast protests. With the arrogance of
youth, I overestimated my role and underestimated the winning
combo of timing, support, and sheer luck. Regardless, all feedback
had been positive, and I expected the review to be more of the same.

I entered my newly hired white manager's office, nervous yet confident. She had an already wilting fern on the dusty windowsill across from me I remember wanting to water. She carefully picked up a small stack of papers from her desk, at which point nervousness overtook confidence — it started to feel like a court ruling and I was in the prisoner's chair. There were so many pages! Quickly skimming over the impacts on the thousands involved in the successful campaign I was responsible for organizing, she went on to cover my skills. Colleagues bemoaned the fact that I rarely joined them for lunch, at the same time sharing that I was too sensitive and shouldn't take things so personally. I was confused by the seemingly contradictory messages to spend more time with people while also being less like myself. They said I was quick to act but was sometimes too aggressive. Also confusing, as this could be the definition of any political organizing job. Mostly, though, as she read word by word, page after page of "feedback," each comment transparent as to who had said what, I felt myself starting to drown in a past where the judgment of my classmates was so annihilating I dissociated in order to survive. This exercise felt like more of the same — it was traumatizing. I only heard the negative parts of what the manager said, and each word whirled faster and faster until there was a tornado in my head, sucking in everything positive. Not yet able to tell my own story, this feedback became the story I assumed must be true about me. I walked out feeling imprisoned in a monstrous version of who I was, but I couldn't find an escape hatch to claw my way out. That night I was up for hours dealing with the aftershocks of shame in the only way I knew how: a tray of desserts and ice cream, followed up by fingers forced down the back of my throat. Over and over.

In hindsight, this well-intentioned, supposedly anonymous feedback exercise triggered old circuits of racial trauma and rejection. Studies now show we register social pain in the same circuits in which we experience physical hurt. Physical injury, though, is easy to recognize and everyone supports you. Emotional pain, on the other hand, is less visible, so it leaves one feeling more isolated. Whatever trust I had built in the people around me and the organization I worked for was simply blown away. It took me more than two decades and years of therapy to recognize it wasn't the feedback that was the issue (or not entirely) but the fact that it stripped away the one place I felt safe. I felt powerful at work, but it was clear "powerful" was not the same as feeling empowered. For that, I had to dig deeper.

Moving into my new office on the new third floor of our newly renovated house occurred at the same time I became CEO. The first room I'd had entirely to myself since moving in with Shakil and having children was both workspace and sanctuary. On the far wall I hung a handwoven bag my grandmother made in the 1960s — dishcloth liner and all. A lower shelf held a silver-plated horse given to me on my sixth birthday in Tehran after the party was cancelled because I came down with the mumps. And, of course, books — so many books! — lined floor to ceiling, stacked around the outskirts of the room. Sliding doors opened onto a rooftop balcony, and beyond that there was a view of treetops and open sky. Everywhere I looked, each static object reflected back a different expression of power.

My grandmother's handbag reminded me of the power of intergenerational love.

The ballet-pink couch and Persian carpet were there because I had the economic power to buy them.

The silver horse and other special objects came from the power of friendship and community.

The trees outside the window stood upright because of solar power; the lights inside relying on electrical.

And everything in the room, including me, depended on the constant power of gravity to hold us in place.

Power is everywhere, each of us held in place by a million visible and invisible privileges. It's perhaps the greatest human challenge to learn to see and use the power we have access to in loving and generous ways, rather than to get stuck seeing only the power we don't yet have. Power literacy is in its infancy, but if we could learn its language, if we could wield it to support our fragile webs of connection, *what might be possible?*

If my dream job wasn't enough to feel powerful, then where to go? I decided to head in the opposite direction to changing the world around me and, instead, focused on healing myself. Soon after leaving the campaign job, I travelled down to one of the largest yoga and spiritual lifestyle centres in North America. While there, we were assigned to a cohort of ten to go through a four-month Buddhist lifestyle program. Each week, we met for a couple of hours for a group check-in, where we were asked to notice our breath, sensations, and emotions, and to share what we felt comfortable with. The only rules were to be in the moment with what we were feeling and to listen silently, non-judgmentally, and with compassion.

Growing up one of the only Brown kids, always the outsider, often socially shunned, left deep trust wounds that made vulnerability threatening. It was a revelation to realize I could stand in front of a crowd of hundreds, megaphone in hand, leading a political chant, but I felt terrified to say anything personal in front of this small group. Each week I took ever increasing risks. I started with "My hands are sweaty and I'm having trouble breathing." As the weeks went by and I shared layer by layer, the silent acceptance

I was offered by others allowed me to *hear* my own story and pull it free from the web of shame it was caught in. Perhaps I wasn't a horrible twisted human being but merely another human being trying to figure things out. Maybe it wasn't me that was the problem but external conditions that made it hard to be myself. Toward the end of my time at the centre I took the biggest vulnerability risk of my life. I told the group I struggled with bulimia, that I made myself binge on food and throw it up and, more, that I was finally committed to dealing with it. This group of strangers held my darkness and cheered me on toward the light. What gets broken in community can only be healed in community.

We can't truly see the power or privilege we have until we deeply know our own story, until we take our own side. If we can't grieve for the hurts, disappointments, and harm that we carry because of the abuse or misuse of power by others and the ways in which we *were* the victim, then we will always be stuck in that singular version of ourselves. A few years ago, I decided I would offer a two-day leadership retreat for women of colour, a group collectively known to face multiple barriers in the workplace — often referred to as the concrete ceiling. About fifty women signed up across a wide array of racialized and Indigenous backgrounds, some who had never attended a professional learning course before.

We started off in a glorious bubble of connection and solidarity around shared experiences of racial and gender discrimination. But then toward the end of the second day, the storm began. Trust issues and more deeply held trauma were touched, and there was a struggle between Brown, Black, and Indigenous women as to who had it harder, quickly tearing apart our fragile common ground. Anger at not having access to social power in broader society came out in this space where it was safe, causing these women to replay the harm enacted on them by passing it on to others. It was heartbreaking to witness. When we make one part of our identity — our race or gender or religion — *everything,* we become unbalanced and are more prone to wield power harmfully, using our wounding to justify wounding others and often ourselves in the process. Accumulated pain gets internalized as depression or externalized into revenge or rage. Both are fragile sources of power because one is so easily thrown off balance. Swinging between both extremes for years, I know that underneath both expressions is a deep desire for the world to hear and acknowledge the damage created by forces outside our control. We can't move out of feeling like a victim until we can see, tell, and own our story of legitimate victimhood.

But the thing about becoming the boss is that people care less and less about your intention, and focus more and more on your impact. You can't be in leadership and be the victim.

I wish I could justify or downplay mistakes I make as CEO by pointing instead to the discrimination I face because of my identity. The reality of systemic racism and sexism never goes away, and women of colour are on the receiving end of power downgrades in almost every environment, all the time. Yet I can't be held hostage to this part of myself where I experience less social power because it can blind me to other aspects where I hold tremendous privilege. It was a turning point to grieve all the ways I had little access to power — safety, acceptance, comfort, and belonging — after immigrating here from my country of origin, but I couldn't remain stuck there. I kept taking risk after risk, stepping into new roles and environments, weaving in new information about myself through and in relationship with others. My story became more complicated than being a victim of external forces. I realized I also have the advantages of education, of English as a first language, of being able-bodied, but also of internal traits such as being efficient, creative, and intuitive. These ingredients had to be added to the story I told about myself. The more aspects of ourselves we're aware of, the more adeptly we're able to hold the power umbrella over other's heads, keeping them dry rather than poking them in the eye.

*

I've just finished another team meeting focused on future business strategy: too many clients, offerings, products, ideas, directions, and not enough time, people, or resources to make it all happen. I have strong feelings about the options available. I can *feel* the vision that wants to come forward and as CEO I figure it's my role to guide the process. After the meeting I walk out of my office and suddenly realize I'd inadvertently interrupted again, more than once.

"Damn!" I think, then, "That's my job though! I have the background for this, and I've spent a lot of time thinking about and mapping out the plan!" Then back to, "But I keep making the same mistake. Maybe I'm better off not being the CEO!" And with those words, the child in me stomps down the stairs. It takes me a while to recover equilibrium.

The most important leadership ability of all is the power to see our own power. I look in the mirror and give myself a talking-to: "You can't give yourself a break when you have the most power. It's your job to consider your impact and clean up your act because you have the greatest influence here. Get it together, girl!" But it's not quite that straightforward. Being able to face up to one's own mistakes or personal deficits isn't just about a momentary pep talk, it's opening the power tool–bag and remembering that vulnerability can be safe. It's taking a few moments to connect to breathing, to allow the triggered emotions of frustration and shame to pass through the body, and to also allow myself compassion. I've had to *work* to get to a place where I not only recognize my strengths but know them in my bones. Perhaps I also created this business so I could feel safe growing in my leadership role, because there is so little room out there in the world for women (especially women of colour) to make mistakes. Connecting to my superpowers of passion, storytelling, creativity, intuition, and visioning, doesn't make taking in constructive feedback easier, it is what *allows* me to take it in without it taking over.

Even with my identity as someone who goes against the grain of those who continue to hold leadership roles, I don't want to become hardened like so many whom I've had contact with. I remind myself that I want to be a bridge, not a fortress. This behaviour of interrupting is not the only truth, it's *a* truth. I remind myself I am a story with many possible endings. It's a blessing to recognize that through all the challenges and barriers I've always come back to the cracked mirror at the bottom of the well, thrown in my coin, and yelled into the void: "What's my part here? What do I need to learn? How can I do this better?" I know it's possible to master the art of giving feedback to ourselves first: gently, gracefully … and honestly. Over time, this practice can lead us to the truest feeling of empowerment where we are able to look at who we are, good and bad, warts and beauty marks, horns and halos, and ultimately decide who we want to become.

I like to think that feeling powerless for so long humbled me enough not to re-create those threatening or stifling conditions here, for those I oversee. I've learned the hard way that like anyone, I have the power to *choose* whether to abuse my authority or whether to use it to build up others. Asking for feedback and giving it to myself is the strongest antidote to misusing power. It's become the medicine I take to grow my own leadership, and although I sometimes hold my nose and swallow it down quickly, it's good for me and for everyone around me. Acknowledging the newly acquired power I have in my role as CEO, and putting in place deliberate checks and balances, allows our diverse team to evolve into something new together. I'm now part of a collective story.

*

The amount of positional power, identity power, power based on our personalities, power based on our expertise, power due to our appearance — and the list goes on — that we have access to ultimately determines our belonging quotient, whether we're part of the innermost in-group or living a few neighbourhoods over. Some of us aren't even in the same country. Yet we're all stuck fighting our way toward or defending our territory within the promised land, clawing our way out of the barrel of irrelevance, wanting so desperately to know our lives leave behind some meaning. It's seductive to look forward, to notice how much further ahead others are, rather than to look backward to notice everyone we're leaving behind. When we can be honest enough to recognize our unique power signature — the places where we have privilege as well as where we don't — we give ourselves a choice to use power kindly and bravely, smoothing the path for those behind us rather than battening down the hatches. Power fluency prevents us from making others' lives a living hell.

The truth is that we all drop down to earth with a hidden jet-pack of superpowers. The stronger our power, the more challenging it can be to see it in ourselves. It's apparent to me when I'm teaching, coaching, or facilitating — a person's joy revealed in the quick flash of an infectious smile; their courage to reveal an honest but challenging truth; the deep compassion shown in reaching out across differences to offer support. We all have these innate abilities, and though some of us have to hunt harder than others to find them and fight harder than others to risk letting them shine, when we do we're *breathtaking*. Feedback isn't meant to dim our star power but rather to help send us shooting through the dark night of this human journey, illuminating those around us with the light of our sheer brilliance.

If the more than six billion humans on the planet were thus supercharged, I wonder what a collective channelling of power could look like. Think what it has already looked like: the civil rights movement, the women's rights movements, Arab Spring, Black Lives Matter. Human meteor showers, all. Each time a group of people gather together to amplify their feedback on what is no longer serving, the world changes. All strides toward the betterment of people's lives have come through individuals stepping into power, standing against the misuse of power, changing other lives through the collective harnessing of power.

As for me, at the end of the day, I just fucking love being the boss. This daily deluge of chosen feedback — from myself and from others — is slowly clearing the dross off this five-pointed star.

STRENGTH

"Oh, Mama," my daughter admonishes in loving rebuke, "that's not how you make the bed."

"You don't shuffle the cards like *that*." Or, "That is *not* how that song goes." She sounds like an eighty-year-old in an eight-year-old body.

In these moments, I will sometimes respond irritably, "Please don't talk to me like that!" Her condescending tone picks at old hidden scars.

She innocently asks, "Like what?"

"Like you know better than I do," I retort.

Then she is often silent because we both know she has no basis for denial.

And I will suddenly chortle out loud because I will remember I am being confronted by my own eight-year-old self in the flesh — the way she trusted her own knowing over others and took for granted the freedom to assert it.

I don't want my daughter to lose this power, and in these moments she reminds me that I haven't lost this quality either.

"Oh, Arion," I will say, "bossy just like your mama!" and we'll giggle away together, laughing so hard at times it feels like we're splitting a hole in the fabric of the universe so more like us fall through to earth.

POWER

The sign blinks in my right field of vision: *50% Off Summer Shoes*. I pause and decide this is too good an opportunity to pass up.

Stepping through the door, I'm greeted by the tall white man standing behind the counter. "Hi," I respond, smiling briefly at him as I move toward the shelf on my right. No time to waste in this footwear paradise! As I'm weighing the shape and height of the different options and mentally trying them on, I sense the man's presence behind me.

I half turn toward him. "I'm fine, just browsing," I say.

"Okay, no problem," he responds.

I wait for him to move away, to leave me to my sartorial imaginings. He moves a foot closer.

I start wondering if he is racially profiling or coming on to me, an abuse of his racial or gender identity? Perhaps this is a strange tactic to elicit pressure to make a sale. Either way, I'm uncomfortable. Feeling my defences rise, I turn fully this time to face him.

"I'm okay on my own here," I say carefully, with a slight edge in my tone. "I don't think you need to stand so close to me."

A look of irritation flashes across his features before he retreats back across the room. It still feels awkward a few minutes later when I ask to try on a couple of sandals and he silently fetches them for me.

We endure a few throbbing minutes in silence until, finally, I decide to engage him in conversation. How long has he worked here? Does he live nearby? Has he watched the latest Euro cup soccer game?

As we're moving side by side toward the cashier for me to make my purchase, I ask him what the return policy is. He doesn't answer, so I repeat the question when he's standing across from me behind the counter.

"Sorry, I have hearing problems," he confides. "I can't tell what someone is saying unless I read their lips."

I feel a wave of embarrassment wash through me. How quick I was to put him in a category of overbearing white male without checking my facts.

"I'm so sorry!" I stutter out. "I wish you'd told me earlier."

I leave the shop thinking how power is not absolute but relative to who we're in relationship with. And even if we don't have as much social power, it still doesn't give us licence to be an asshole to those we perceive as having more. I took a shortcut in there; I could have been kinder.

Power is always present in our interactions, but the form it takes changes, and it's our job to stay awake to its guises so we may bridge rather than break. I did both today, I think to myself. Though this is my area of expertise, I am continuously humbled by learning.

Who we underestimate reflects our own limitations to belonging.

WELCOME

Arion throws a shoe across the room at her younger brother in frustration. I rush out of the bathroom, zipper undone, and yell, "Enough! Go outside … NOW!" This is only the twentieth time I've cajoled and demanded, yet each time the fighting has only increased.

To emphasize that *this* time I am really serious, I shove the conflict culprit — the remaining gingerbread house wall, tube of icing, and bowl of candy — into a shopping bag and then hide the whole thing in the garbage. Neither child is happy with me. Arion stomps out of the house, pulls out her bike, and pedals away down the street in righteous defiance.

I inwardly acknowledge my response falls far short of my ideal parenting standards, yet I'm late to meet a friend, so knowing Shakil is in the house I quickly pull on my coat, decide to do damage control later, and depart in the opposite direction.

Fifteen minutes later, as my friend and I are strolling down the street, Arion bikes past on her way back home. "Hey," I call out to her. She favours me with a grumpy look. "Say hi," I call. It's a golden rule in our house that we always welcome people with a greeting. I'm shocked when she turns her stony gaze forward without responding and bikes on.

Embarrassed by her behaviour, I hurriedly explain the gingerbread house fallout, finishing with the explanation, "It's unusual though for her not to respond with a —"

"Hello!" we hear shouted from across the street. Arion has biked back to us. She waves at my companion, and then directs a frown at me before pedalling away again.

Despite her frustration with me, I smile, my shoulders relaxing back into place.

I know the crumbled gingerbread house will soon be forgotten, yet I trust the practice of welcoming others will stick around. We all fight with each other, it's what comes afterward that counts. Belonging is built through the strength to hold onto kindness, especially in the face of anger, to remember that we are connected even when it doesn't feel like it and that our feelings are never an excuse for exclusionary behaviour. Especially, it's remembering that each stranger is a relationship waiting to happen.

My daughter may be young, and she may still throw shoes, but she showed skills far beyond her age today.

SOOTHE

The plane has landed and bodies are popping out of seats all around me. My attention is caught by the Brown couple across the aisle as their baby starts to cry once again. The mother is wearing a sari; they appear South Asian to me. Both are nervously attempting to pacify their little one: rocking, patting, and finally placing a soother into the small mouth. I inwardly smile in relief that it is no longer me in this position.

Unexpectedly the man in the row behind me snarls, "Fuckin' immigrants. Can't even keep their own child quiet!" Suddenly, it's hard to breathe. I watch as people turn away, busying themselves with their luggage, believing that ignoring these words of violence will somehow diminish their impact. Out of the corner of my eye, I see the couple bow their heads lower, shrinking into their seats.

Anger rises in me at this tall white man's entitled aggression, targeting this family who are clearly vulnerable. But I catch myself and remember that I am not responsible for saving this situation. I remember I don't want to lose my humanity confronting another human. I remember that how I respond will land on the family in front of me.

I turn and look him in the eyes, forcing myself to smile. "Do you have children?" I lightly inquire.

"Yes!" he declares loudly. I cringe inside, feeling like we are two figures projected onto a screen, everyone around watching intently.

"I have children, too," I say. "Travelling with them was hell."

"Well, use a fucking soother! It's not hard," he persists.

I force a laugh as though we are trading insider parenting tips with each other. "I don't think it's that simple. I think you might be forgetting how hard it can be."

He ignores me, but he shuts up and starts packing his stuff. People around us look the same as moments before, woodenly going through habitual motions, yet I can tell the ice is broken because somehow it's easier now to take a deep breath.

I turn around once again and attempt to make eye contact with the mother holding her child or the father with his hand on her shoulder. Neither of them are looking at anyone else, keeping their eyes fixed on the tiny, newly hatched face in front of them.

I stand for a moment longer, hoping they can feel someone stood for them today, hoping the man behind me remembers that I held his humanity intact today, hoping there will come a day when more of us feel we can stand as shields in moments such as this.

I remember that belonging is not bestowed but cultivated, requiring the courage to uphold both sides of the bridge, to act as human soothers in dangerous times.

10

OCEAN INTELLIGENCE

We've been at war with an invisible virus for two years, fighting against Mother Nature herself. It's hard not to feel battle weary. At least once a day, I find myself stifling a desire to scream at a rotating carousel of villains responsible for this ongoing, sad state of affairs, other times at the whole sorry fallibility of human beings — how we unfailingly make multiple, worse messes from a single mess.

Stirring cream in my coffee each morning, staring at ice-cased branches on neighbourhood walks, fighting for the just-right position for my head on the pillow at night, I'm increasingly desperate for hope — the fragile belief that the future can be better than this present. Yet, in the absence of organized faith as the age-old hopemaking machine, where do we go? How do we cultivate a sense of belonging to this life when so many of our usual supports are being stripped away? Wearing masks, spending all day on a screen, having limited contact with each other day to day, now year after year feels like we're becoming an alien species — alien to the lives we used to live, alien to the people we used to be, alien to each other. Perhaps in this time of crisis all we can do is trace back to where we came from and learn from what has allowed us to survive.

Escape

A handful of years ago, a New Zealand octopus miraculously made headlines: Inky, the size of a soccer ball, managed to escape her tank in the National Aquarium through a tiny gap, scamper 3 metres across the floor, squeeze through a 150-millimetre hole, and drop down all 50 metres of drainpipe to reach the ocean. Scientists were not surprised. Most famously, octopuses are known for these kinds of radical breakouts through holes as small as a coin. They are also the oldest creature on the planet, constant inhabitants of our first and common ocean home. We share ancestral DNA. I think how we are like our tentacled brethren, floating in this sea of sorrow, squeezing ourselves into the tiniest possible holes (or URLs) to escape these dark days. The octopus learned to survive by becoming a master escape artist.

I can relate.

The first escape was from everything. In the flight from Iran after the Islamic revolution of 1979, we left behind family, culture, land, belongings, and life-savings. We left a hole in time, between the Shah leaving and Ayatollah Khomeini establishing full control. No more jumping over fires in the schoolyard for the annual *Chahar Shanbeh* festival preceding Persian New Year, eating delicious *Sangaak* bread and plates of loaded *Sabzeh* (greens), and running amok yelling as loudly as we could at every social gathering. We had our lives, but we lost the people and routines that governed them.

The second escape was from God. After moving to Canada, Mum's British Methodist roots deepened. I believe it was her way of coping with our transplant. Neither she nor my father were able to regain their professional status because their credentials didn't translate, and on top of this, she was saddled with adjusting three kids to an unfamiliar and often hostile place. She took us faithfully to church every Sunday. We were the only Brown kids there, and Mum was one of few single parents to attend. Being a sensitive kid, and church being the only place where belonging seemed within reach — at least in theory — I leaned right in. When I was nine years old, I asked my mother, "How do you feel God?" She answered, "You just ask Him to come into your heart." I went across the hall, kneeled on the bright orange shag carpet, and did just that. And I felt something, a comforting presence insulating me from the most damaging harm of the racism and rejection surrounding me. This comfort lasted until I was twenty and my roommate came out as gay. According to conventional religious strictures, heaven was positioned as an elite members' club open only to certain identities. I couldn't reconcile a loving God with an exclusionary afterlife, so I left. I had my principles but lost my safety net.

The third escape was from politics. In my early twenties, I worked for a political party, believing that changing policies would create more space for people on the margins. I moved to Ottawa to organize a national campaign aimed at protecting democratic rights and creating economic fairness. Between Parliament and the leaders of various national organizations, it was a homogeneously white world. I agreed to represent some colour by appearing on our very white organization's brochure. I was passionate about bringing in more diverse representation, though I didn't know how to articulate all the reasons why. In 2001, Brown men who came from the same part of the world as I did flew a plane into a tower, and my world changed again. People of Middle Eastern descent were targeted and bullied out of people's ignorance and fear. I looked to my political community to offer support and allyship and realized few were feeling the depth of fear I was. Steps toward building bridges with Muslim and Middle Eastern organizations weren't happening in a meaningful way. I was burned out, so I chose to leave rather than fight what felt like an endlessly uphill battle toward inclusion. I left with a deeper awareness of systemic inequalities but lost my ideal of the kind of close-knit community required to move us into a better future.

The fourth escape was from New Age spirituality. After leaving the social justice realm, I travelled and spent a few months at a spiritual lifestyle program at one of North America's largest retreat centres. It was, again, mostly white people, this time dressed in expensive hemp/cotton yoga gear that cost the same as half a month's rent. I enjoyed the yoga, thrived on the meditation, but couldn't find a place for myself within the *sangha* (community). The book *The Secret* was big at the time and popularized the idea that if you believe something strongly enough you can make it happen. I was shocked by otherwise intelligent folks believing we have the power to attract or repel our circumstances. "What about child soldiers in Rwanda? Do they choose their fate?" I asked in one workshop, flushed in the face. I carried this frustration at privileged non-attachment, at the ignorant "we're all human" excuses and attempts to spiritually bypass suffering, through all the subsequent yoga and mindfulness sessions I attended there and in the years beyond. No wonder people of colour — who incidentally founded many of these communities' lineages — were missing. Eventually, I stopped inhabiting these kinds of spaces. I gained insight into how to manage my emotions, but I lost trust that people of colour would ever be at the centre, despite their role in creating the practices.

The fifth escape was from working for others. After spending my twenties and half of my thirties working across the nonprofit and public sector, I came to see how few organizations lived up to their values, how leadership was so often lacking. Power was always the insider currency, but it was rarely acknowledged so it came out in mostly unhealthy ways. So many organizations felt like dysfunctional families with parents laughing and smiling outside of the home but abusive inside it. Almost no organizational leaders at any level of government were people who looked like me. It was a revelation how much of the institutional leadership remained white folks of a certain class, so far from representative of our population. From working across a breadth of organizational structures — nonprofit, academic, government, coalitions — I experienced how human systems worked and what it meant to create change within them, but I lost any desire to work for another white leadership team.

Over the decades, I left clubs and teams, groups and relationships. At the faintest whiff of rejection, cliquishness, or insider-outsider dynamics, I would escape. But any pattern of behaviour comes with a cost. The price for leaving is isolation. You get stuck with yourself, inside your own head. Escaping may be a means of surviving, but what happens when there is nowhere left to go?

Destruction

When the octopus is threatened and leaving is not an option, they have various tools to ingeniously adapt to their environment. Octopuses are masters of disguise. On a recent visit to our local aquarium, our family held a fifteen-minute "spot the octopus" competition. None of us won, though we realized afterward that she was hiding in plain sight, right in front of us — the same white-and-black spots as the rock she was lying on. The octopus can also disguise itself by shifting shape. When under threat, it can change the size of the blood vessels under its skin from small ball-like bumps to large sword-like spikes, a kind of three-dimensional, instantaneous morphing effect that scientists still know little about. But when an octopus gets really stressed, when escape is impossible, she will enter a state of autophagy, where she will start eating her own limbs. In foreign environments where adaptation is too stressful, she will choose death.

When I couldn't escape the biggest commitments — marriage, children, and a business — I started eating myself alive from the inside out. It was shame. Shame is the emotion that tells you not that you've done something wrong but that you *are* wrong, an emotion all too familiar from childhood. My circuits were primed. Shame wouldn't have been visible on the outside; I was far too sophisticated for that. But inside, I started panicking, and over time I could pull myself out less often or easily. I felt ashamed for not conforming to professional WASP norms — too outspoken, determined, and bossy for a Brown woman. I hated "mommy and me" play groups, with the careful white mommy conversations that I could never squeeze into. I wasn't organized or ordered enough to be a good domestic partner, which caused conflict in my marriage.

Without any readily available escape hatch, I chewed on my own shortcomings. I picked at my body, forcing myself to binge and purge occasionally. I picked at my skin, sometimes to the point of bleeding. I mentally picked at myself, getting migraines, sometimes to the point of involuntarily vomiting. I felt so lost in waves of shame that at times I'd cancel dates with people. Even the thought of being in close proximity felt like I might drown. Once, a white acquaintance's retaliatory response — "You ask such strange questions!" — to what I thought was a friendly query resulted in a couple of hours doubled over and sobbing in a pitch-black basement bathroom. The thought of being called out as strange in front of a group of people felt so threatening it caused a mental health crisis. Here, once again, was proof that I was not worthy of being *accepted*. Studies show humans fear rejection more than death. It does not surprise me. When I got sucked into that darkness, I imagined ways of cutting my wrists or slicing my belly. Shame is hell locked inside the mind and perhaps the biggest legacy of racism.

Shame is also an addictive emotion. It took me a while to understand that shame itself can be another form of escape. Feeling bad or guilty about what I wasn't living up to meant that I stayed absorbed in my own experience and was no longer present to what was happening around me, or even aware of the potential for transformation. While writing this piece, I had a dream that I was at a large social event. Someone interviewed me on the purpose behind this book, but despite how articulate I was, I couldn't communicate my message. I was on a panel with other writers and started asking more and more questions because I felt I didn't know enough to speak myself. As I went down the stairs, a man walked past, looked me up and down, and uttered under his breath, "Zero." I felt the word land like a noose around my neck. Waking up soon afterward, I could feel the lingering aftershocks of shame. But as the dream circled in my mind throughout the day, I realized that zero is also the circle, the snake chasing its tail, the story without end. Zero is the fool in tarot, representing a new beginning. I wondered if the dream wasn't reflecting shame but resilience. One thing I've always been good at is starting anew.

Regeneration

This pandemic is forcing many of us to confront ourselves. Mental health is a parallel battle being fought in billions of heads all over the globe. Crisis forces one's hand. Our survival patterns will either have us eating ourselves alive or force us to transform. But cannibalism is not the end of the story for the oldest sentient being. The octopus may eat its own limbs, but it can also regenerate any part of its body. Destruction is not the end of the story; the possibility for regeneration is.

This pandemic forced me to reach out for medication to help with anxiety and depression. That helped. I reached out again and got diagnosed with ADHD. Getting diagnosed for something in mid-life is a roller-coaster ride. While it put many things into perspective, it had me tracking and re-tracking all those millions of steps through hallways of the past (as if I needed more thoughts to process!). Was grappling with feelings of zero-ness a result of the trauma of racism, the genetic predisposition of ADHD, of being hypersensitive, or maybe something else? I didn't have an answer, but what I did have was a way of understanding certain behaviours and their impact. This is the purpose of a diagnosis: it puts a face to the confusion, a pattern to what can feel like panic, a conclusion to a chapter that seems never-ending.

Naming something can be the start of being able to make it better. But it isn't the only way. Seeing myself only through the lens of ADHD or trauma or my role as a CEO can so easily become their own forms of oppression. Not every truth applies in every situation, nor, if present, are truths equal in any situation. If there is a conflict at work or at home, sifting through the causal factors is a process, not a one-size-fits-all answer. Were life that easy! I am so much more than a diagnosis, or my skin colour, or what I do for a living — any human being is galaxies beyond the names we give to them. This is what regeneration is — we are always growing, and that growth can sprout from multiple sources is where hope lies.

The pandemic is a diagnosis. Our planet is sick. But *we* are also so much more than this — a species known for our strength, resilience, and intelligence. Our answers to what we struggle with are also not going to come from one place, one framework, or one solution. Religion can't answer for growing poverty gaps. Political systems don't peddle in spiritual meaning-making. Psychotherapy is still lacking in understanding the impact of racism. Comfort may be found in one way of understanding the world, but belonging is not. Belonging inside ourselves or the world we live in is found through the weaving of many perspectives. Diversity is our saving grace. It's the ocean between us that holds us together, resilience arising from our multiplicity, and the most ancient of creatures that have something to teach. Two-thirds of the octopus's brain are in its limbs. Eight tentacles hold more information than the singular head. When one limb is taken away, another grows in its place.

Evolution

Octopuses have a reputation of being closest to an alien species because their DNA operates differently than the genes of any other species on the planet. While human DNA is fixed from the moment of birth, the octopus can update its DNA in response to its environment. Rather than passing genes from one generation to the next, they can alter their DNA quickly as needed. An octopus is incredibly adaptable when presented with a challenge. There's an octopus named Rambo that learned how to use a camera, a skill humans take time to master. They can successfully pry open the lids of childproof pill bottles and other sealed containers. Octopuses are surprisingly intelligent and recognize different people even when dressed in the same clothing. They can also appear almost psychic at times — Paul the octopus famously predicted the FIFA world cup winner a staggering twelve times out of fourteen. This jellylike cephalopod reminds us that growth can look fundamentally different from what we're used to: the ugliest, oldest, and slowest of creatures demonstrating miraculous feats on par with what humans are capable of.

Perhaps being different isn't a curse but a blessing because being different forces us to take risks, allowing us to find fundamentally new paths forward. To survive future pandemics (and their equivalent) we need to cultivate more alien intelligence, the opposite of what we're used to. Put Indigenous leaders in charge. Create naps for workers in the middle of the day. Measure growth by GBP — Gross Belonging Product — rather than by revenue earned off the backs of those whose lives we consider expendable. Move like an octopus, where feelers at the margins bring in more valuable information than what's at the centre, where three hearts beat instead of one. Find the humility in remembering that there are more questions than answers in this world still full of mysteries.

At almost half a century, I've evolved into a different person than the one I used to be. Now, when I feel the urge to escape, either in presence or spirit, I remind myself, "Staying is the practice of faith that this can get better." I've learned that without committing myself, there is nothing to belong to. Sometimes I still choose to leave, but it's no longer the default.

These days shame is a rare visitor and when she does arrive, I am able to carry her gently rather than hold on for dear life while she's yanking the reins over rocky terrain. I recognize that turning in on myself is an old defence mechansim that no longer works and is no longer necessary.

Now, when I feel myself getting too rigid, lost in my own fear or despairing of humanity's ability to solve the problems facing our planet, I remember that hope is a choice, a renewable resource. I close my eyes and remember moving in water, flexing all those intelligences or ways of knowing. I remember the ocean, not this single body, holds the answers. I remember to bow to the circle, surrender to the power of zero, and, like the fool, harness the courage to let things start over again.

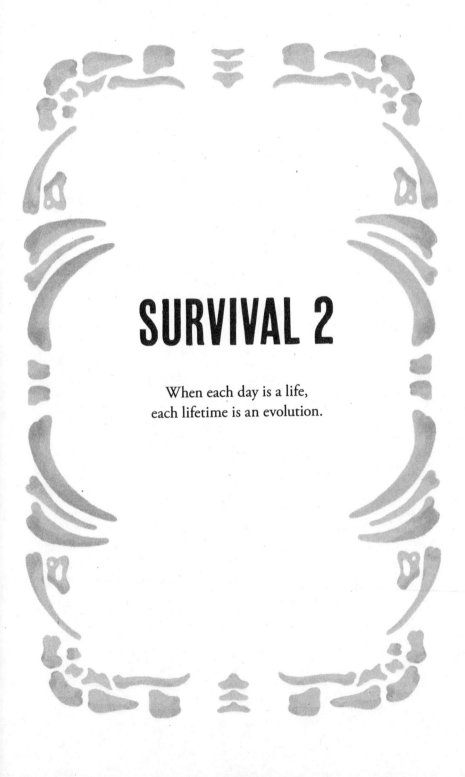

SURVIVAL 2

When each day is a life,
each lifetime is an evolution.

EPILOGUE

Dear Daughter,

Fanning the flames of belonging will be the challenge of your generation, for mine has forgotten what it is to take for granted that we deserve to feel safe in our bodies, to have connection within our communities, and to have a home here on earth.

There's a theory that all life originates from meteorites crashing into the earth, bringing with them the necessary DNA precursors. If this is true, then we are *all* immigrants here, foreigners from some distant star. We are creatures of dust, small bits of matter so fragile yet so fertile. Put us in a sunbeam and you'll see us start to shimmer.

I've spent most of this life desperately wishing I was a different speck of dust, wanting to be *better* than what and who I am. I've wanted to be thinner. I've wanted to be whiter. I've wanted the right accent, the right clothes, the right boys to notice me. I've parcelled up pieces of my soul and given them away — indiscriminately — to people who I thought were on a pedestal so high that if I just worked hard enough I'd earn the right to spin in the air beside them.

I swallowed the idea that I was less than, an aberration, and that I had to pay a high mortgage for my right to exist on this planet. This is the original poison: that somehow human worth can be ranked according to skin colour, amount of money, gender, sexual orientation, or religious beliefs. If you remember nothing else, Daughter, please know you do not have to earn your right to feel worthy — belonging is the birthright gifted to us all. Our bones remember this for they are made of dust.

When you were three, I walked you across the field to daycare, and as we passed another parent with a child about your age, they yelled across to you, "Hi, Arion!" I twisted around suddenly as you responded in kind. How could you know somebody I didn't, I wondered in surprise. Up to this point your new acquaintances and mine were one and the same, as you went nowhere without me. It was the first time I confronted the truth that you are your own dust mote, beside yet completely separate from me.

You will find your own journey through this world, sometimes on the ground, sometimes in the sky whirling above the masses. You will experience light and darkness, belonging and rejection, a feeling of home and, other times, profound isolation. Love all of it. Planets don't exist without whole galaxies to contain them; humans don't exist without generations upholding them. Draw on the strength of the ancestors, and learn to pay their courage forward.

You are star matter, Daughter, let yourself sparkle. And may this book be a sunbeam just for you.

ACKNOWLEDGEMENTS

The pandemic was a container for this book on belonging, and my family was a container for me. The pandemic also reminded me, as for so many of us, of the importance of family. My children, Arion and Koda, drove me crazy every day, and every day saved my sanity as only children can. I could not love or admire them more. Shakil, my life and business partner, inspires me every day with his steadfast love; belief in me and the power of these words; and integrity in who we are as a couple and as a family. He always walks his talk. Thanks for continuing down this dusty road with me.

I also want to thank my family of origin, whom I love very dearly: my mother, Janet; dad, Jamshid; stepmother, Zari Joon; and my younger siblings, Fari and Shah. We've walked such a long journey together and continue to do so. Also, Shakil's parents, Saeeda and Anil, who care for our children like only grandparents can and inspire me with their constant love and generosity.

No book comes into being without guardian angels, and I've certainly had my share. Thank you first and foremost to my editor,

Noelle Allen, who was an instant fan of *Breaking the Ocean*, my first book, as well as of this one, and she faithfully cut my words down to size. A huge thanks as well to Kwame Scott Fraser, publisher at Dundurn Press, who is one of a small handful of BIPOC publishers in North America and who said yes to this book instantly. Laura Boyle at Dundurn designed the gorgeous cover, which I told my daughter came a close second to hers. Also, thanks to Alyssa Boyden in publicity and Robyn So as copy editor. To everyone at Dundurn, thank you for backing me. Caroline Starr was also an early and brilliant editor of most pieces here — I will always owe you a beer.

Writing is such a solitary pursuit, but I call myself lucky to be buoyed by the many friends, colleagues, and clients who light my days and inform who I am and what I write. This book wouldn't exist without all of you. A big shout-out especially to my colleagues at Anima Leadership, especially Alex Krosney and Felicia Falconer for your expert support. Kristen Roderick, thanks for editing even more words in the form of the *Soundwaves of Belonging* podcast. Annie Simpson, Judy Rebick, Barb Thomas, D'Arcy Martin, Sandy Yep, Parker Johnson, and Vanessa Reid, thanks for showing up at different times in the writing process and cheering me on.

And, lastly, to my adopted nation, Canada, an imperfect but mostly wonderful place to live. I don't take living here for granted. Every day I expand my sense of belonging through this landscape and the people who inhabit it.

ABOUT THE AUTHOR

Annahid Dashtgard (M.Ed.) is co-founder and CEO of Anima Leadership, a socially innovative company offering a compassionate approach to racial justice. She's a renowned inclusion leader, author, and speaker with over twenty-five years of experience working in the trenches toward social change in public, private, and nonprofit sectors. Dashtgard started out organizing national campaigns but now focuses on shifting consciousness, one conversation, one compelling story at a time. She's the author of the bestselling memoir *Breaking the Ocean: A Memoir of Race, Rebellion, and Reconciliation* and the host of the podcast *Soundwaves of Belonging*. She loves nothing more than a spicy cocktail, a new book, and an afternoon nap, ideally in that order.